PRAISE FOR
KIM ADDONIZIO

"Kim Addonizio writes like Lucinda Williams sings, with hard-earned grit and grace about the heart's longing for love and redemption, the kind that can only come in the darkest dark when survival no longer even seems likely."   —Andre Dubus III

"Like Anne Lamott . . . Addonizio seems to sense how to pull back from sentimentality, be it with humor, honesty, or clarity of vision."
—*Los Angeles Times*

"Addonizio tackles tough subjects—unequipped mothers, the loss of love, mental illness—with unflinching clarity, lyricism, and humor."
—*San Francisco Chronicle*

"Kim Addonizio's imagination is like a runaway train under perfect control. Nuanced, shaded, and unshaded, her poems are bold, brave, respectful of the darkness, perfectly pitched, and virtually every one reverberates with a kind of wild tenderness."   —Thomas Lux

"Kim Addonizio's poems are stark mirrors of self-examination, and she looks into them without blinking."   —Billy Collins

"Searingly beautiful, evocative, and surprising. Kim Addonizio is a master . . . in the best tradition of Robert Coover and Angela Carter."
—Katie Crouch

"Wonderful . . . A streak of dark humor, colored with a tinge of pathos, infuses her best work."   —*The Oakland Tribune*

"For all their fleshiness, stiletto stylishness, and rock-and-roll swagger, Addonizio's finely crafted and irreverent poems are timeless in their inquiries into love and mortality, rife with mystery and ambivalence, and achingly eloquent in their study of the conflictful union of body and soul." —*Booklist*

"Addonizio's honesty and self-knowledge will pierce you to the core."
—Carolyn Kizer

PENGUIN BOOKS

Bukowski in a Sundress

Kim Addonizio is an award-winning author of fiction, essays, and poetry. She has received numerous honors for her work, including the John Ciardi Lifetime Achievement Award and fellowships from the Guggenheim Foundation and the National Endowment for the Arts. Her poetry collection *Tell Me* was a finalist for the National Book Award, and she has won Pushcart Prizes for both poetry and prose. She is also the author of two popular writing guides for poets, *The Poet's Companion* and *Ordinary Genius*, and teaches and performs internationally. She divides her time between New York City and the Bay Area.

ALSO BY KIM ADDONIZIO

FICTION
The Palace of Illusions
My Dreams out in the Street
Little Beauties
In the Box Called Pleasure

POETRY
Mortal Trash
My Black Angel: Blues Poems and Portraits
Jimmy & Rita
Lucifer at the Starlite
What Is This Thing Called Love
Tell Me
The Philosopher's Club

NONFICTION
Dorothy Parker's Elbow
(edited with Cheryl Dumesnil)
Ordinary Genius
The Poet's Companion (with Dorianne Laux)

BUKOWSKI
in a
SUNDRESS

Confessions
from a Writing Life

KIM ADDONIZIO

PENGUIN BOOKS

PENGUIN BOOKS

An imprint of Penguin Random House LLC
375 Hudson Street
New York, New York 10014
penguin.com

"How to Succeed in Po Biz" first appeared in *New Letters*; "Pants on Fire" in *New Ohio Review*; and "How I Write" in *Booth*.
"Plan D" was published in *Bad Girls: 26 Writers Misbehave*, edited by Ellen Sussman (W.W. Norton, 2007); "A Word of It" (as "How I Found Poetry") in *Red Thread, Gold Thread: The Poet's Voice*, edited by Alan Cohen (Ravensun, 2009); and "Necrophilia" in *Dirty Words: A Literary Encyclopedia of Sex*, edited by Ellen Sussman (Bloomsbury USA, 2008). "How to Succeed in Po Biz" later appeared in *Pushcart Prize XXXIV*, edited by Bill Henderson with the Pushcart Prize Editors (Pushcart Press, 2009).

LIBRARY OF CONGRESS CATALOGING-IN-PUBLICATION DATA

Names: Addonizio, Kim, 1954- author.
Title: Bukowski in a sundress : confessions from a writing life / Kim Addonizio.
Description: New York : Penguin Books, 2016.
Identifiers: LCCN 2015042338 | ISBN 9780143128465 (paperback)
Subjects: LCSH: Addonizio, Kim, 1954- | Women authors, American—20th
century—Biography. | BISAC: BIOGRAPHY & AUTOBIOGRAPHY / Literary. |
LITERARY COLLECTIONS / Essays. | BIOGRAPHY &
AUTOBIOGRAPHY / Personal Memoirs.
Classification: LCC PS3551.D3997 Z46 2016 | DDC 818/.5403—dc23

Printed in the United States of America

1 3 5 7 9 10 8 6 4 2

Set in Abobe Caslon

DESIGNED BY KATY RIEGEL

for my tribe

Contents

Plan D   1

How to Succeed in Po Biz   9

A Word of It   17

Necrophilia   21

Children of the Corn   25

Are You Insane?   33

How to Try to Stop Drinking So Much   41

Pants on Fire   51

Flu Shot   57

All Manner of Obscene Things   69

Not Dancing   79

How I Write   85

Simple Christian Charity   87

Best Words, Best Order   97

Don't Worry   103

Bukowski in a Sundress   109

Cocktail Time   115

Penis by Penis   119

DOA   129

How to Fall for a Younger Man   139

I ♥ New York   155

What Writers Do All Day   165

Untrammeled   169

The Process   177

How to Be a Dirty, Dirty Whore   185

Space   195

Acknowledgments   205

Bukowski
in a Sundress

Plan D

I T   W A S   T H E   L A S T   frenetic night of the big conference, and a few hundred people who weren't too old or too hungover had gathered to party down one last time in the hotel ballroom. Under the requisite mirror ball, most of the attendees stood around while a few wild souls gyrated to oldies from the sixties. The DJ kept exhorting the crowd with comments: "You cats know how to rock 'n' roll, don't you?" "All right, everybody, here's a blast from the past!" It could have been a conference of urologists or ghost hunters or nanoscientists, but it happened to be a conference of writers, many of whom were overmedicated professors released from their small-town colleges for a few days of intensified drinking, schmoozing, and airing of professional resentments.

I was wandering the ballroom, stoned out of my mind, bothered by a left eye that was watering profusely from an accidental squirt of champagne earlier—the yeast in champagne, apparently, is the irritant—and I'd had too much scotch besides. The pot and alcohol were courtesy of my friend Jeff, whom I was now looking for. I was at that pleasant, slightly hysterical stage of being moderately fucked up, where the most appealing course of action is to get quickly to the next stage, that of near obliteration.

Once an aspiring professor, Jeff was now the personal assistant to a famous writer; mostly, he interacted with the assistants of other famous writers. When Oprah called, her people talked to Jeff. It was a lucrative gig, so when it came to intoxicants, Jeff could afford the best. I thought of him as my supplier. Every time I walked out of a panel (Strategies for Reaching Underserved Communities in the Creative Writing Classroom) or reading (Tribute to a Newly Dead Writer We Didn't Pay Much Attention to Until Now) or hospitality suite party (Free Booze for Important People and Attractive Female Grad Students), he would be there to catch my eye and say, grinning, "Wanna go to my room and get high?" No doubt he hoped to get lucky, but all that would happen was we'd smoke his hallucinatory pot from his blue metal pipe and drink copiously from the several bottles lined up on his hotel dresser-cum-wet bar and gossip about other writers' love lives and who was publishing where, and then we would fall awkwardly silent until I staggered up from one of the matching orange chairs and reeled back out to the next scheduled event.

But now I'd lost Jeff, so it was time for Plan B: finding someone in the ballroom I recognized who could buy me a watered-down drink at the cash bar near the dancers. I caught sight of an associate professor named Lori, resplendent in a one-piece skintight tiger suit, but she was busy grinding her pelvis to "Louie Louie" in the direction of a much younger man. Good for Lori. I took another survey of the dance floor, dropped Plan B, and headed for the hotel bar upstairs. Plan C: find Jeff and get more pot and alcohol. Plan D, if it came to that, was to hit up a stranger at the bar.

I find it's important to have a plan, to keep some sense of control, some belief that even if there's no order to the universe, even if it's all chaos and darkness, you can navigate your way through it with some existential dignity. At this time of night I figured there would be plenty of drunk men to choose from, and I had on my tight black jeans and high-heeled combat boots and tight Betty Boop T-shirt. In other words, fish in a barrel. I was pretty sure I wouldn't need Plan E: go back to my room, throw myself on my orange bedspread, and cry uncontrollably.

The hotel bar turned out to be jammed; there were so many conversations filling up the room I couldn't even hear the light rock station that was usually playing. This was where all the hungover writers had sensibly repaired to after the evening's readings and receptions. I spotted the back of Jeff's head. Oddly, he had on a different shirt, and he seemed to have let his hair grow out a bit in the hour or so since I'd seen him last. Still, I strode right up and punched him on the shoulder.

Okay, so it wasn't Jeff. The man who turned around had bright green eyes—or maybe they were blue? The main thing, the important thing, was that he was dreamily attractive, and clearly as happily surprised to see me as I was to see him. Neither of us could believe our luck. I explained about Jeff as I glanced around the room, making sure he really wasn't there to bother me, while my new friend ordered me a vodka and cranberry. In about ten minutes we had progressed from flirtatious conversation to kissing while the men to our right muttered drunkenly to each other about the luck of other guys.

"How come this never happens to Cookie?" one of them said.

His friend had been calling him John, so maybe Cookie was what he had named his dick. I could have told him why it never happened to Cookie—he was holding forth on safe sex, for one thing, dropping witticisms like "rubbers are for tires"— but I was busy exploring the inside of my new friend's mouth with my tongue. His name was Ken; it was stitched in red on his jumpsuit. He'd just gotten off work, which involved installing refrigeration units or something equally, blessedly foreign to literary life, and he had come to visit his sister, who tended bar here. Seeing how wasted I was, she began serving me straight cranberry juice—not that I noticed. Ken mentioned it after I came back from a fourth trip to the bathroom off the lobby.

When the bar closed, I led Ken up to the eleventh floor, where I was sharing a room with another writer, who'd known me long enough to have forgiven me already for more than one similar transgression. I hoped she was in a forgiving mood again. I cracked open the door; the room was dark.

"Hi," I whispered. "I brought a man home. Do you hate me for it?"

From out of the darkness came her benediction: "No, Kim," she said. "I love you for it."

It didn't occur to me until later that this comment might have been ironic.

We tried to be quiet. But gradually, as things got under way, Ken and I got louder. We laughed while he tried to get my boots unlaced in the dark and unpeel my jeans. We laughed when I knocked over a glass on the night table—the drink I'd brought with me from the bar. When his roving hands discovered my pierced navel, he said, "I've never met anybody with an earring in her belly button." More laughter.

In the next bed, my roommate turned over and sighed. Another turn, another sigh. Each was a long exhalation that might have meant she was turned on, or that she had had enough of my slutty ways and would never speak to me, let alone room with me, again. It was impossible to tell, and it wasn't the time to do a check-in with our feelings. I was too busy feeling Ken's tongue move to where his hands had been.

We stayed up until almost dawn, and then he left without either of us exchanging cards—something I'd been doing with complete strangers for the past three days. Not that Ken would have had a card, but I could have given him mine, and maybe asked for his phone number. I could have called him up and asked whether he thought the universe was essentially random, or possibly invisibly organized according to some divine plan, and he could have responded with an appropriately hopeful metaphor from the world of refrigeration; I was casting him in the role that Robert De Niro played in the movie *Brazil*. But it was more like *Last Tango in Paris*, or the beginning of it, anyway, before the Marlon Brando character falls in love with the young French girl and becomes needy and pathetic and wants to know all about her. Ken and I had an understanding. We came, we stripped, we conquered loneliness for a few hours. That was it. He put his tongue down my throat one last time, and then we parted.

The alarm woke me a couple of hours later. My head hurt so much I could barely move. But I had to catch the hotel shuttle to the airport. My friend—possibly now my former friend—had already left for her flight. She probably hated me for keeping her up all night, and for whatever horrible crime I had committed and forgotten; there seemed to be a few gaps in my memory. I couldn't remember, for example, whether Ken and I had actually consummated our encounter, or just fooled around. I looked for a telltale shriveled condom or torn-open foil square: nothing.

I had to pack and get on a plane, and I was going to puke at any minute. I stuffed everything into my suitcase and duffel and made it downstairs in time for the airport shuttle. I kept my sunglasses on and hoped I wouldn't throw up on my fellow writers, who appeared not to notice that I could barely sit up as they discussed their programs, their students, their teaching loads, their hoped-for sabbaticals, their publications, their grant and fellowship applications, their literary journals, their lives that apparently, at least at this moment, did not involve lustful nights with refrigeration installers.

On the plane at last, I kept my sunglasses on and found a free row of seats where I could lie down. I vowed never to drink again, if only I could make it home without throwing up. I vowed never to pick up another man in a bar, ever, even if I didn't keep my first vow and found myself in a bar, stoned and drunk with one eye watering from champagne. And if I did end up with somebody, I was going to carry a concealed recorder and play everything back later so I would know for sure whether I had compromised myself.

I did remember a few things. Ken told me he'd been left by a woman a couple of weeks before. He had come to the bar depressed, thinking about her; the idea of ever being with another woman, at that moment, was inconceivable. He was suffused with her, her, her. Her name was Kristi, with an *i*—he spelled it twice, to make sure I got it, while fumbling in the dark with the hooks on my leopard print bra. Sitting on the plane, traveling away from him, Ken Somebody, at hundreds of miles an hour, I could still feel his hands sliding down my back and smell the sweat I'd licked from his armpits. I was sick and sour-breathed, and in the white of my left eye a red blotch had appeared and was spreading like some miniature crimson star violently being born. I was a writer who would never be a tenured professor, a throwback writer, the kind who came to conferences and drank too much and committed inappropriate acts with inappropriate people instead of chatting up somebody who might help my career. What career? I couldn't really connect that word to anything I'd ever wanted as a writer.

Curling up under a couple of thin airline blankets, taking deep, shuddering breaths, I thought about how stupid writers conferences were and how I never wanted to go to another one. I thought about poems I wanted to write, and about Ken and his girlfriend, Kristi, and about how long it had been since I'd been with a certain man who had drained the shot glass of my heart, slammed it on the bar, and walked away. Hurtling over towns and cities and bedrooms far below, I remembered that just before Ken left me, he called me an angel, and I realized then that, for him, at least, I was.

How to
Succeed in Po Biz

MANY ARE THEY who harbor the burning desire to become successful poets and rise to the top of their profession. To see one's name on the cover of a slender paperback, to have tens and perhaps even dozens of readers, to ascend to a lecture podium in a modest-size auditorium after being introduced by the less successful poet, who is unsure of the pronunciation of your name—these are heady rewards. And beyond these lie the true grail: generous grants, an endowed chair at a university, the big money that will allow you to write and remodel your kitchen while freeing you from reading the incoherent ramblings of inferior wannabes. How can you realize your dreams? Follow this step-by-step advice.

First, receive some measure of recognition as a writer. Publish in a few literary journals of small circulation, and then publish a book or two with a struggling nonprofit press and receive a pittance of an advance on modest royalties. This is step one. Step one is not as simple as it sounds. Think of a little baby, of how long it takes it to raise its head without a hand cradling it, then how long to flail its arms about, until the happy day it manages to roll over of its own accord. Think of the months of crawling; multiply them a hundred times or so, and you will have some idea of the difficulty of step one.

Yet babies do stand, and eventually walk, and soon no one thinks anything of it. Of course, some babies will never learn to walk, and if you are one of these unfortunates, it is true that you may never reach step one. If so, be grateful that you don't face the challenges of those who must make their way on two legs. Cats and dogs, opossums and peccaries, rabbits and armadillos and scarab beetles—these are all more content than humans, and all are equally valuable—are, in fact, beneficial to the earth rather than a blight upon it. Humans who are writers are a devastation. Writers plunder, excavate, and strip-mine without regard for the consequences to others. They suck their loved ones dry of vital fluids, revealing their deepest fears and yearnings. They expose the most precious secrets of their friends and families, then take all the credit and get all the applause. But if you can manage to stand, and are willing to be such a vampire, a succubus from the realms of depredation and darkness, read on.

Step two is to win some small, local awards, and then, after half a lifetime of literary labor, finally to be nominated for a major award. For the ceremony at which the winners will be announced, fly to New York City with the miles it has taken you seven years to accrue. Bring your boyfriend with you, even though the two of you are breaking up, because you are afraid to go alone. Spend an afternoon having your makeup professionally done for a taping of a Barnes & Noble interview in which you say things like "If you want to be a writer, you must simply persist." Say this while looking directly at the camera, like an actor in a movie who has dropped all pretense of being a believable character, like a politician feigning sincerity while laying the groundwork to rip away every freedom you hold dear. This interview will never air. Try to get through the next twenty-four hours without washing or even touching your face, so your makeup will be intact for the ceremony.

At the ceremony, held in a big hotel, stand beneath an enormous black-and-white photograph of your face. The photo is very flattering, and perfectly lit, like a shot of a designer handbag. In front of it, your actual face looks like a bad knockoff. Smile. Later you will weep in the empty ballroom—everyone else will be at the cocktail party—while your almost ex-boyfriend (all wrong for you, not to mention fourteen years younger, but what an amazing body; you will never feel those muscled arms holding you again, sob, weep, weep) goes around to each table loading up on the leftover stacks of free books. Later still, you will watch a revered male writer, honored earlier with a Lifetime Achievement Award, relieve his compromised old bladder in a potted plant in a corner of the lobby. When asked by a concerned publisher if he needs help, he will respond, "What, do you want to hold it for me?" and you will weep again. Not because of the frailty of human beings no matter the scope of their accomplishments, but because when the winner of the major award was announced, it was not your name that was spoken by the celebrity emcee, not your folded-up speech thanking your mother that was heard by the hundreds of people pushing the berries-and-chocolate dessert around on their plates.

It is crucial not to win the major award, because then you might feel too great a sense of achievement. Be a finalist, but not a winner. This will keep you forever unsure of the scope of your talent, and you will be able to continue the habits of excruciating self-doubt and misery that stood you in such good stead during the many years you received no recognition at all. Notice that all around you, people of little imagination and even less heart are being honored with prizes, with obscene sums of money, with publications of their execrable twaddle in prestigious magazines like *The New Yorker*. Hold fast to the simultaneous sense of moral superiority and abject failure this observation inspires.

At this juncture, pay close attention to your e-mail. (Your account name should be chosen from among these: hatemyjob, writergrrl, rimbaudsister54.) Check your in-box compulsively to see if anyone wants to offer you money to give a reading or workshop. These offers will be few and far between, so you will find yourself reading spam to justify running to the computer every three minutes. You will begin to seriously consider adjusting the size of your nonexistent penis, or giving your bank account number to the stranger in Nigeria offering to split his inheritance with you. You will become fascinated by strange strings of words such as *bullyboy bangorcumberland jehovahmonetarist antares driftdeadline embeddable ephesusmyrtle*, and wonder if you can use them somehow in a piece of writing. Ordering a large, unaffordable prescription of anxiety-relieving drugs will be a constant temptation. Resist that temptation, and steal your new boyfriend's Xanax instead.

Once or twice a week, drink a little vodka mixed with lemonade in the middle of the day, while your boyfriend is at his real job, making four times as much money as you. You are a poet, after all; a little something to take the edge off is allowed. You work part time in order to write, and lately you aren't writing much of anything. What you do write, you realize, is crap, garbage, shit. That major award nomination, which once seemed to promise such a heady future, was in fact the apex of your career. From here you are on a downhill slide. Since the nomination, you have received numerous form rejections, no grants or fellowships, and several fan e-mails from people who clearly meet the legal definition for insanity. These are the people who want to date you. They have pored over your poems and concluded that you will not only share your naked body with them, but also read their demented poetry and thrust it into the hands of editors they are sure you must see socially, or how else would you have become a recognized writer in the first place?

Occasionally, the subject heading of the e-mails will say, OFFER OF READING or WE WOULD BE HONORED . . . Open these e-mails and respond immediately. Don't wait the few days you give the insane fans so that they will assume you are a busy, wildly successful writer with no time to correspond. Accept with alacrity all offers that contain the magic word *honorarium*. Reject the others, no matter how nice and gushing the offer, because you are likely to end up sitting through a three-hour open mic during which someone will sing, someone else will break into cathartic sobs, a third person will drum, and the technician recording the evening will step out from behind the camera to read his first-ever poem that he just now wrote, he was so moved and inspired. When formulating your rejection, it is acceptable to lie. If the reading is nearby, respond, *"I'm so sorry, but I have a previous commitment."* If the reading is farther away, say, *"I'm so sorry, but I was recently injured and my doctor has not cleared me for travel."*

Once a bona fide, i.e., paying invitation has been extended, try to obtain as high a fee as possible. Tell yourself you are worth every penny, but secretly feel the way you did when you were on food stamps: other people need and deserve this more than you. Feel anxious about the upcoming trip because you hate to travel. Feel anxious because you are basically a private person and can't live up to the persona that is floating out there in the world acting tougher and braver than you. You are a writer, after all, and prefer to be alone in your own house with your cat. You don't really like your fellow humans, except for your boyfriend, whose stories and mannerisms can be usefully stolen and put into your writing. When he traveled with a carnival as a young man, he learned to eat fire and put a nail up his nose. Sensibly, he left the carnival to work in sales, while you suspect that you have become a sideshow act, a fake mermaid shriveling in her tank, uselessly flipping her plastic tail.

As the event approaches, ramp up your level of anxiety and focus on these specific possibilities: The presenters will not have obtained a single copy of your books to offer for sale. There will be an audience of three in a six-hundred-seat auditorium. You will miss your ride from the airport and end up lost in a strange city late at night, in the winter rain, trying to climb in the window of a private citizen's apartment you have mistaken for the university guest residence. Two teenage girls will come to the window and ask you for cigarettes, and then their redneck father, who thinks you are a prostitute, will show up and tell you to get the fuck away from his daughters and drive you back out into the freezing elements. These things have all happened to you, so your anxiety will be well founded.

Go ahead and have a little more vodka with lemonade and get slightly drunk by dusk. Try to write a few good lines and then give up in despair. Tell yourself you are foolish, feeling terrible when you have actually been asked to share your work with other people. It is the work that you love, and sometimes you even get paid for it. Tell yourself you are lucky, that people envy you. Tell yourself this is what you toiled and sweated your whole life to be able to do, and now you are doing it, and above all, don't be such a goddamned little baby.

A Word of It

WHEN I WAS young and living with my parents, my father still living and my mother still young, though I was too young then to understand how young she really was—when I was a girl and did not yet have a girl myself—when I was a young girl, my lovely living father owned a copy of the *Rubáiyát of Omar Khayyám*, translated by Edward FitzGerald. The book had a soft brown leather cover, and its title was in gold, so it felt exotic. My father read to me from that book: "The Moving Finger writes; and, having writ, / Moves on: nor all your Piety nor Wit / Shall lure it back to cancel half a Line, / Nor all your Tears wash out a Word of it." And in his voice, which I found beautiful, my young and beautiful father said, "A Jug of Wine, a loaf of Bread, and Thou," and I could nearly taste the bread's sun-warm crust and didn't yet know the taste of wine or what it meant to have a beloved. That book, those words, that afternoon when we were all so young—that was possibly the start of it for me, that glimpse of a possible rent in what I thought was the whole fabric of life. Portal, threshold, door in a tree.

In my twenties, after I'd left home in Bethesda, Maryland, and moved across the country to San Francisco, I sat reading in an attic room and was dumbstruck by something that was called poetry: a fragment of Plath, though I can't remember which poem it was, only that some internal tectonic shift made me know I needed this thing, needed the way it changed my experience of life. I had fallen into plenty of novels as a child, and through them had entered places I preferred to the one I found myself in looking up from the page. Narnia was far superior to Bethesda. I loved the magical pull of other, parallel worlds: traveling through the universe in *A Wrinkle in Time*, or sailing a model boat with Stuart Little. Part of the pleasure I took in *Stuart Little* came from my father reading me the story at bedtime, though he had a macabre way of wrapping things up when he was tired of reading, or decided I should get to sleep. "And they all fell down in a pool of blood," he joked, "and that's the end of the story." It was an ending from classical tragedy, but the next night everyone would be back where they belonged, ready for further adventures.

But I hadn't quite realized there was yet another parallel world that would place me under a spell so profound that more than thirty years later I have yet to wake up.

That poem I first encountered in San Francisco must have been in *Ariel*, gateway drug for so many young women coming to modern poetry for the first time. The book has since been lost. Soon after reading it, I would begin to lose my father. That year he suffered a stroke that partially paralyzed him. I flew back to visit him in the hospital, and read him my first poem. He listened with his eyes closed, and I thought he might have fallen asleep. When I finished, he struggled upright in bed, pointed a shaking finger at me, and said, "Write!" Then he fell back exhausted on the pillows. He recovered somewhat, but soon more strokes sent him to a nursing home for a year. I spent the morning he died rereading his letters, many of which had encouraged me to give up music, which I was pursuing at the time, and to write instead. Though he was a sportswriter, he occasionally wrote poetry and had a deep romantic streak.

Over the next years, the town I grew up in would virtually disappear, every building downtown razed and replaced except for a ramshackle wooden structure that still advertised vacuum cleaners for sale. My mother would sell the house we grew up in, and grow old, and I would understand something about this whole process, though not really. I would struggle to feel the deep joy in the mystery of change, not simply the terror and loss, and poetry would help with this. I would discover other poets, fellow singers and raconteurs and black-humored travelers, and find my way to writing more poems of my own.

Once on a visit, before the house was sold, I found that copy of the *Rubáiyát* and brought it home with me. It now has hundreds of other volumes, some of them mine, as companions. There is a framed broadside of one of my poems, a poem about desire and a red dress, written after I had tasted the wine, had found and lost the beloved, was struggling still to understand. I can still see my father sitting on the edge of my bed, holding the book in his hands, reading to me.

In the fifteenth century, the Sufi poet Rumi wrote, "In truth, everyone is a shadow of the Beloved."

"And Thou / Beside me," my father read, "singing in the Wilderness."

Necrophilia

NECROPHILIA IS A TERM that is commonly misunderstood.
You probably think it means being so attracted to dead people that you skip the dating part and go straight to their
place with a little wine. You probably imagine walking into
a cold, smelly basement with awful feng shui, spritzing the
hell out of it with a good air freshener, and boinking away.

I misunderstood this particular word until one day, a
year or so after the breakup of a long-term relationship, I
realized it must be meant as a *metaphor*—that is, representative or symbolic of something else. Just like the Bible. When
Jesus said to become as little children, he didn't mean, for
instance, to throw your burned pork chops on the kitchen
floor of the apartment you rented after letting your ex keep
the house. He didn't mean you should stomp on your dinner,
screaming and crying. As for the wine that is Christ's blood,

if I may offer an *explication*—which is the same as an expla-
nation, only more complete. What it means is: go ahead and
drink the whole fucking bottle of pinot if it makes you feel
less lonely. Just so we're clear on that.

What necrophilia is, really, is this: sexual obsession for
men who are incapable of having a real relationship because
they have no heart in their chest cavity. What they have is an
empty socket that will electrocute you if you try to get close
and touch it or maybe just point a flashlight that way to see
what's wrong. These men can't have feelings for anything but
girl-on-girl porn, American League baseball, and the thought
of the fortune they are going to make when their ship, which
is lost at sea and listing badly with several leaks in its rotting
hull, finally comes in.

Exempli gratia (aka "e.g.," which means "free example," like
in the better markets where you can get cubes of cave-aged Gru-
yère and pieces of artichoke sun-dried tomato pesto sausage and
make a slim but upscale meal of it): in my *single*, i.e., oppressively
solitary, state, I developed a crush on this dead guy—of course,
before I realized he was dead. That's how you get in trouble: they
look so lifelike. He was charming and talented, and about a
week after we met he e-mailed me "U r beautiful," and that's
pretty much all it took. I'd been alone for a year at that point,
and—how shall I phrase this correctly?—living alone is a *hellish
nightmare* (i.e., *id est*, a dream arousing feelings of intense fear,
horror, and distress: e.g., you feel as though you are trapped in a
small, dark crawlspace with someone who is hitting you repeatedly on the forehead with a hammer) from which I am still trying to wake up (*cf. nonketotic coma, vegetative state*).

Tell me *U r beautiful* and I'll probably fall for you, dead or alive.

Anyway, after this guy and I saw each other three times and I gave him two prolonged *courtesy sucks*—I am not one to tire easily, but even I was reaching the limits of my politeness—followed by one *bouncing of the Brillo*, or *dancing of the buttock jig*, without ever experiencing my own *petite mort*; after he didn't call for two weeks only to tell me, when he did, about playing paintball with his friend who sounded moronic, well, then I finally realized I had encountered a bona fide dead guy and that I might be suffering from necrophilia. This was confirmed by *The American Heritage Stedman's Medical Dictionary*: I had an "abnormal fondness" for being in his presence; I had "sexual contact with" *and* "erotic desire for" his body. I was, in short, a textbook case. I had all the symptoms. No cure was mentioned.

I consoled myself with the thought that while I was definitely sick, he was definitively *dead*—asleep, belly-up, bloodless, blooey, checked out, cut off, gone, paralyzed, spiritless, stiff, torpid, unresponsive. So maybe he had carried me to bed once and was a really good (in fact, excellent) kisser; to him I was only a pair of breasts and a nice ass in tight jeans, heavy combat boots, and a cute hoodie. The e-mails I agonized over, trying to hit just the right tone—provocative nonchalance—were living side by side with the pervy forwards passed along by his infantile, also deceased or at least comatose friends. Smiling snowmen with carrots for dicks. Jokes about hillbillies. *"Why do they always have sex doggy style?" "Because their womenfolk don't like watching NASCAR upside down."*

Hahaha.

When I realized how *stupid* I'd been—that is to say, how brainless, dazed, foolish, naïve, and obtuse—I wanted to put a stake through his heart.

Then I remembered he didn't have one.

A corpse, let's face it, is pretty much empty. The blood gets drained out, the organs are harvested, the brain is plopped into a jar for the benefit of science. It's not even really a body, only the outside of one. A lot of them look pretty sexy when they're embalmed: beautiful, unreachable models of imperfection. To a certain kind of person, they may present a challenge, a hope, a profound messianic desire: to raise the dead, to lift them from their graves and rented rooms and broken couches, brush them off, and dress them in better clothes.

If you are a necrophiliac, you know exactly what I mean.

They are irresistible. They shimmer with energy. In the chill air, they seem to form clouds of breath that take the shape of the possibility of true connection.

Children of the Corn

AFTER A DAY of travel—taxi to train, train to airport, two flights—I arrive at a small midwestern airport to spend a week at a small midwestern college as a Visiting Writer. It's another three and a half hours from the airport to the town, late at night, in a howling, full-on blizzard. We creep along in a big boat of a car with no proper tires or chains. The snow is horizontal, blowing across the empty cornfields with nothing to get in its way. Sometimes it changes direction and aims straight at the windshield. My hostess slowly navigates over patches of deepening snow and ice.

I imagine us slaloming into a ditch, trapped upside down in the middle of nowhere, quickly buried by snow, our bodies turning to frozen tuna steaks. In the spring we will thaw and smell bad. Someone will throw us away. I wonder if my obituary will make the *Times*. If my friends will have found the homemade porn movies I made with a long-ago boyfriend and burned them, as I requested, before my daughter discovered them. If it's too late to beg my hostess to turn around so I can make the long journey home and wake up tomorrow safe in my own bed, honorarium be damned. I would pray, if that was something I did; instead, I stare into the storm, willing my mind to stop saying, *Fuck, fuck, oh fuck.*

"Fuck, oh fuck," my hostess says aloud, sounding more bemused than afraid, and my mind freezes over.

IN OUR ONE-ON-ONE consultations, to which each undergraduate student has brought two poems for critique, I tell all the girls—most of them are girls, except for one gay boy and another of indeterminate sexuality—that they will find their power through writing. One girl's eyes fill with tears. Another goes ahead and starts weeping; it has all been too much, this talk of imagery and dangling modifiers, the difference between *lay* and *lie* and the suggestion that the boy and girl dancing like fairies at the sea's edge, where the stars are smiling and dancing on the water, might not be her true material. I end our session by giving her a long hug. Pat, pat, pat. These are fucked-up, damaged little girls. They have built their shrines of pain, and I am saying, in the gentlest way possible, under the guise of discussing their poems: *Smash those false gods! Open your wings and fly, my tender, trembling little birds— fly like fairies, like rainbowed butterflies! You are free!* They blink at me with their sad, tormented eyes. *I can't move, you idiot,* they seem to say. *Don't you see how overwhelming it all is?*

And I want to tell them that, yeah, as a matter of fact, I do. I've had a chance to look around. You are stuck in this nowhere, economically depressed town, where the stench of pig factory farms wafts over rotted porches and caved-in barns. The roadsides are littered with smashed cats, with the corpses of skunks and deer. You've had a shitty public education, and you are completely unprepared to make your way in the world. After you graduate, the Walmart up the highway will likely swallow you after masticating you slowly. And you think you may want to be poets. God help you, my children.

AT A POTLUCK dinner at the dean's house, one guest, clearly desperate to maneuver the conversation away from the usual turgid departmental shoptalk, launches into a story about a couple she used to know. The man, whose name was Jellybean, rode a Harley and had skull beads woven into his beard. The girlfriend had PROPERTY OF JELLYBEAN tattooed on her ass. The guest talks engagingly about the night she sat in the front seat of a car between the two of them, holding a frozen Butterball turkey on her lap, as Jellybean's property proposed a three-way. You can tell she is a fiction writer and that these people and the turkey will end up in a story one day. Already I've made use of them, because I am also a writer, because this is what writers do. We are alert to the possibilities life sets before us. What potential in a man named Jellybean! When my hostess says, "Fuck my life!" in response to the fiction writer's story, I am elated by her turn of phrase, scribbling notes on the inside of my brain for later use. "When we had our sexy time," she says of an ex-boyfriend, and "He was such a cuckoopants." I swoon with bliss.

My good humor is increasing by the minute. I was dreading this gig, as I dread most unknowns, especially if they involve a rural area of the country. And here I am having a wonderful time. Is there something wrong with me that I am enjoying this experience, so alien to my usual sophisticated city pleasures? For here there is no theater, no open café after sunset, and not a single decent restaurant. In the town square is a store that sells bridal dresses, the mannequin couple posed with a mannequin toddler, a blond, blue-eyed Aryan in a white tuxedo, holding a box displaying a diamond ring. In another store are rows of hideous prom dresses of a size that can only have been made for giant drag queens. There is a knitting store and a gift store with gaudy scarves and handbags and jewelry, and a store that sells only lightbulbs. They fill the entire display window. In the summers, my hostess tells me, there are also jars of honey.

I'M BEING PUT up for the week in a bed-and-breakfast, a lovely old Victorian. These places, despite their surface charm, are a horror to me. No privacy, no pay-per-view movies on TV. In the morning, around the communal table, there are strangers whom you must confront before dispelling the miasma of dreams with quantities of coffee. The B&B owner is a sixtyish German woman I'll call Helga. One night, when I come in from dinner—the evening's festivities here end around 8:00 p.m.—I find Helga in her beautifully appointed parlor with the leaded stained-glass windows, doing shots with her neighbors. She takes a long time to bring up the tea I ask for. Tonight, swacked out of her mind, she is charming, swaying barefoot before me with a tray of tea and cookies. Usually I am a little afraid of her. She has a harsh German voice and runs everything with the efficiency I associate with other, earlier Germans of an anti-Semitic bent. Usually I creep around, trying to escape her notice. Helga makes delicious breakfasts of quiche or eggs Benedict or eggs and bacon, always with a little dessert cup of yogurt with fresh blueberries, strawberries, and tiny pieces of pineapple atop toasted muesli. She serves muffins, and pastries with delicious icing. Out of fear, I eat everything she brings me.

FOR OTHER MEALS, in town or at someone's house, I eat homemade chocolate cake, sweet potato and hominy tacos, guacamole, tamales, beans, a huge portion of fish and risotto, overdressed salad, chicken tortilla soup gooey with cheese. I wash down meals with margaritas, with ice water and Diet Pepsi, gallons of coffee and wine. Within a month of living here, I realize, I would double my hundred and ten pounds and embrace my inner obese, diabetic, alcoholic, middle-aged midwestern gal. She's in her natural environment. I hear her voice, a soft whisper in my ear. *Go forth and eat until you want to puke*, she says, in a faintly German accent. *And don't you dare leave anything on your plate, you skinny little bitch.*

When I'm on the road, I take pictures to text to my friends: a river view from a hotel room, a sculpture in a museum garden, a doe and her fawn nosing the wet grass of a field. I'm nearing the end of my visit and haven't taken a single photo. Out walking in the bitter cold, I pass some folk art created out of the recent snowfall. A snowman stands in the bare yard of a small, weathered wood house, a red bucket set upside down on his head at a jaunty angle, a big Jack Daniels bottle jammed into his snow piehole. His rubber hose of an arm wraps around a snowwoman. Her rubber hose of a right arm reaches for his wooden chair leg of a penis; the other grabs her snow hoo-hah. She is missing a breast. Their eyes are marbles, and they are very blue. *Click*.

At night the train whistle sounds. The train will take you all the way to Chicago if you stay on it long enough. Some of the kids from here will end up there, but not many. The gay student I met is headed there as soon as he graduates. *Get out! Run away!* the whistle shrieks. A bit after 2:00 a.m. it wakes me, in my second-floor bedroom with the red-striped curtain fringes and the view of some denuded, hopeless-looking trees. They do not look as though they have ever bloomed, or will again. This is the hour the kids stumble out from the bars in town, my hostess from the college has told me, crossing the train tracks to get home or back to the dorms. Every year, a couple of them don't make it.

———

WHAT KIND OF life is this? What do people do way the hell out here, in an unincorporated community for which there is no Wikipedia entry, surrounded by limited cable, by country music and Christian talk radio and abandoned farmhouses? They eat and drink too much. They fall in love and marry. They fill empty storefronts with possible light, and with sweetness, and build snow people when they have a mind of winter. When young, they struggle to express themselves through poetry: self-expression, the awful thing whose name we dare not speak, what we who are writers have been taught, and teach, that poetry is not. "Art! Art!" cries the dog of poetry in its doggie bed of plush toys and Tugga-Wubba chews. But here, somewhere in the heart of the cornfields, is a chained dog in a yard of dirty snow, howling like a train whistle, full of longing for it knows not what. And for a brief time, while I'm in residence here, I am privileged to call its name.

Are You Insane?

I WAS TEACHING a day-long poetry workshop in my living room in Oakland. I think it was about metaphor. It would have been the usual stuff: Aristotle, Shelley's apprehension of the relations of things, controlling conceit, metonymy versus synecdoche. Here's a mnemonic: Call someone a douche bag and you're using metonymy. Tell him he's an asshole; that's synecdoche.

Though now that I think about it, the workshop that day was probably focused on revision, as in, Your First Draft Sucks and You Have a Thousand Do-Overs Before You Get It Right. Think of it this way: Build a city, then blow it up to save it. Invent a road to take you far out of town, then start over with a single good brick.

One of my students was a twenty-something guy named Svend, whom I'd met briefly at a writers conference. He was in town from somewhere else and signed up while he was visiting. After the workshop, he wanted to know if I would join him and his friend for a drink.

"Ummm . . . sure," I said. *Ummm* . . . to make it appear that I might have other plans on a Saturday night and was deciding whether to break them, but I didn't have any plans except seeing what was on HBO and Showtime and drinking wine alone and crying, which were pretty much my usual plans whenever I didn't have a boyfriend.

We went to Quinn's Lighthouse Restaurant—Svend, his friend Zach, and I. Quinn's is a laid-back spot on the waterfront in Alameda with an outdoor deck coated with peanut shells. Svend told me he had gone to the University of Montana, after which he'd moved to northern Idaho and then Alaska.

"Wow," I said. "You were really looking for the frontier."

We shelled peanuts from a red plastic basket and sat together through the late afternoon as the sun lowered itself gradually over the docks and the boats like a shining woman lowering herself into a very large, sparkling bathtub. Or maybe like a shooting star on heroin. Or maybe the sun was more of a golden quaalude, slipping down the darkening blue throat of the day.

At dusk Svend tired of whiskey and Cokes and ordered a bottle of champagne. In the way of poets everywhere, we earnestly discussed art and politics. The Herzog documentary *Grizzly Man.* The idiocy of our then-president, George Dubya Bush. Our favorite disaster scenarios involving oil, global warming, and nuclear annihilation. In the way of poets everywhere, we drank heavily. Then I suggested a bar I knew downtown, figuring I would leave Svend and Zach there to get further into their night.

The bar in question was closed, an iron gate across it. This was a clear sign, but having been drinking all afternoon, I had stopped being able to read the signs sometime before. The signs looked fuzzy as caterpillars or fake eyebrows. Immediately we headed down the street to Luka's.

I had sworn off Luka's one night shortly after my last breakup. I'd fallen on the slippery floor trying to dance with some guy who had insisted on walking me to my car, then tried to grab my breasts. I looked around for him now, though I had forgotten what he looked like. We passed through into a back room, music thudding beneath a mirror ball, spermy light motes traveling along the wall. The room was empty except for a couple snuggling on a banquette. I immediately hated them, as I hated all couples for having each other when I had no one. Beyond them was a room with a pool table, where I watched Zach and Svend play against two other guys.

"Hey, she's famous," Svend told them several times.

Writing students are sometimes given to such projections. Being a poet, I am famous, I guess, in the way that a dentist who invented a new method of cementing crowns might be— that is, I am known in my profession. Several other dentists might have heard of me. At a dental convention, they might come up to me and say, "Hey, I really like your work. Sealants, wow. I read your article in the *American Dental Review*." Or maybe, honestly, I'm not all that respected in my profession. Maybe my fame is more like that of the junior high slut. Lots of people know my name and want to screw me, but nobody understands my beautiful, sensitive soul.

"How is she famous?" one of the pool players asked.

I ducked my head and said, "I'm not, really." Then I told them that the three of us tracked grizzlies for a living.

"Oh yeah?" the guy said skeptically.

Trying to make it more plausible, I shrugged. "Well, we don't really track them," I said, revising on the fly. "We're just the ones that tag them."

It was not only bullshit, it was lame bullshit, and we all knew it. We were just a bunch of bored strangers getting drunk around a pool table, our imaginations as impoverished as our love lives. Eventually, Svend, Zach, and I walked out into a deserted Telegraph Avenue and crossed to our respective cars.

"So, goodnight," I said to the boys.

"We need to find a motel," Zach said.

"You're not going back to the city?"

"Nope," Zach said. "I think there was a Motel 6 down the Embarcadero."

I remembered then that Zach had said he was staying in his truck in San Francisco. Maybe he was angling for a place to stay, but I needed to go home and sleep off all the champagne and peanuts so I could be ready to start the next day freshly alone and miserable about it.

At home I took a long shower and then crawled into bed. Pretty soon the phone rang.

"Hey," Svend said, "we can't find a hotel."

I started feeling bad that I hadn't invited them to spend

the night at my place. They were young, they didn't have any money, and Svend had picked up the tab for most of the evening. I was famous and had half a duplex to myself. I even had a sofa bed. "Want to crash here?" I said.

"We're right outside," Svend said.

"I'll let you in." I put my clothes back on to go unlock the gate for them.

I got them blankets and sheets and was about to open the sofa bed, but they wanted to sleep on the floor. That's how young they were. Boys. They weren't old enough to care where they slept. Once I had been like them, a girl pitching forward into the nearest place to sleep, often beside someone I would look at in the morning trying to remember his name. The boys were spreading out the blankets on my living room rug. I got a pillow, gave it to them, and went back to bed.

A few minutes later, Svend came in and lay down on top of the covers, next to me.

"Um," I said.

He reached out an arm and slung it over my waist. I lay there for a minute, knowing I was going to tell him to get out of my bed. He was young—okay, too young. Was he even within shouting distance of thirty yet? His friend couldn't have been much older than my daughter. It was perverted even to think of doing anything with him. He was kind of cute, too. He probably didn't know how old I was. Or didn't care. How many whiskey and Cokes had he drunk? Still, I thought I deserved this much—a long moment with a man in my bed, even if he was a very young, very loaded man who had likely staggered into my bedroom from blind instinct, a starved grizzly wandering into a campsite. I could feel the youngness of him, the maleness, wash over me, and I bodysurfed the small wave that quickly flattened, taking me into shallow water, into the familiar, tar-fouled sand of celibacy.

"You need to get out of my bed," I said to Svend.

"Why?"

"Because I don't want to. And you're drunk."

"You're drunk, too. You want to."

"Nope. Go back to Zach."

"Okay," he said, and left.

A minute later he was back. Lying beside me again. Probably thinking, *Do-over. Writing is rewriting.*

"Svend," I said.

"Are you offended?"

"No." A boy his age had no idea. To get an idea, you had to be a woman who would go out with a couple of kids and spend the evening drinking with them as though she did this all the time, hanging out shooting pool and lying to strangers, spreading her blankets on the rug. Was I offended? No. I was just sorry. Sorry I was no longer interested in sharing a drunken fuck with someone I'd known for an evening. What had happened to my inner slut? Sometime in the last few years, she had shrunk down to nothing. Had I simply passed her through my urine like a kidney stone?

It appeared I was now too mature to get laid.

"Go get some sleep," I said, and he obediently went away again.

Sometime in the early morning I heard him in my bathroom, puking.

When I woke up again, they were gone, the blankets neatly folded. They hadn't even used the sheets. My answering machine light was blinking; I went over and listened to the message.

It wasn't exactly a message. The boys had called me sometime last night, before the call from them that I answered; I must have been in the shower. They had been so drunk they forgot they called me, or thought they'd clicked off the cell phone, so I was privy to their conversation. I wrote it down, word for word, before I erased it.

Zach: Hang a right. No, chill out, it's a cop.

Svend: Whoa, street!

Zach: Jesus Christ, Svend! Take a left. No, go straight.

Svend: I'm going over there.

Zach: You're so close to going to jail. You're closer to going to jail than you are to Kim's.

Svend: That's cool.

Zach: It's over, man.

Svend: It's not over. It's not even close to being over.

Zach: She didn't want us to come.

Svend: Yes, she did.

Zach: She didn't ask us, man.

Svend: Why?

Zach: She knew we were looking for a place. She didn't offer.

Svend: Are you insane?

Zach: Aka, she didn't want us to come over.

Svend: Fuck, we're going there.

Zach: Are you serious?

Svend: We're going to take a left here.

Zach: We're going to fucking hit the Embarcadero!

Svend: God, she's so fucking horny!

Zach: Is she? I dunno.

Svend: Okay, I'm turning around, I'm going to her house, you can get out if you want.

Zach: You have no idea where you're going!

Svend: Fuck! This is insane. There's no fucking Stop sign.

Zach: Where? What?

Svend: Are you insane? Are you fucking insane? There's a cop right behind me.

Zach: Good. I hope you go to jail.

Svend: Fuck you, I'm going over there and you're coming with me.

Then the phone shut off.

In *Grizzly Man*, there's also a recording. We don't get to hear it in the film, only see Herzog in headphones, listening to the idiot who thought he could live in harmony with the grizzlies being torn apart at his campsite, along with his girl-friend. What we imagine—is it worse, or better, than the reality? Aka, being so fucking horny, should I have slept with him after all, and given this story a different ending?

How to Try to
Stop Drinking So Much

REMEMBER YOUR FATHER sitting in MacDonald's Raw Bar, giving you rolls of quarters for the pinball machine and money to buy Whitman's candies and outfits for your Skipper doll at the Drug Fair across the street. Remember how you felt in the dim, beer-smelling bar, listening to him laughing with his friends. His black hair curled on the back of his sunburned neck; his frosted mug caught the little circle of light coming in through the porthole on the door. Remember how the flippers on the machine sent the steel ball zooming back up to carom off the bumpers, the bells and numbers going crazy, colored lights flashing before your eyes.

Hours later, your father drove you and your brothers home down Bradley Boulevard, the car occasionally straying to the wrong side of the road. You always sat rigid in your seat belt, afraid he would hit something: a car coming toward you around a curve, one of the trees that grew so close to the road. Once, when none of you were with him, he landed the car in a ditch not far from the house.

So stop remembering how you loved the heavy feel of all those quarters in your hand. Remember how it felt when the ball shot straight to the bottom between the flippers and disappeared down the hole like a greased rabbit. Remember that every ball ended up going down that hole sooner or later. Think of the quarters running out, the pinball machine unplugged, silent in its sobriety. Tell yourself this silence is what you want.

DON'T KEEP ANY alcohol in the house. On evenings you feel the urge to drink, open the refrigerator several times to make sure there's no white wine hiding in there behind the leftover Thai delivery. In the freezer, discover the two little airline bottles of vodka your friend Elizabeth left nestled behind an ice pack, between a box of coconut fruit pops and a year-old frozen crust for the pie you meant to make but never did. If you were a pie maker, you could be eating some right now. You are sure that with a mouthful of pie, really good pie, you would have no desire to drink. You vow to make some soon from one of the recipes your friend Kate published in her book that included interesting prose poems about fruit and pie along with the recipes. You wrote a blurb for it:

How is a banana like a push-up bra? What's the best way to thicken a berry filling? This book is the answer to the prayers of pie-lovers everywhere. Both whimsical and practical, it will charm your pants off—and your apron on.

Kate's pies are delicious, and you have helped her bake them occasionally. You have yet to make one alone, though, without actually being in Kate's presence. You are a social pie maker, just as you are a social drinker.

Though of course you also sometimes drink alone.

You take out the little vodka bottles. Nothing this cute could possibly harm you. You pour them both into a coffee mug and look for a mixer, but there's no juice, no tonic water, no bitters. You microwave a fruit pop for a few seconds until it's mushy, and voilà: coconut cocktail. Maybe you could write a book of cocktail recipes, you think, but then you'd have to try them out, and that wouldn't be helpful for your current plan, which is to try to stop drinking so much.

You try to remember how a banana is like a push-up bra, but it's been a while since you read Kate's book. What should you call this cocktail? Hawaiian Happiness, maybe. Tropical Trouble. Sex on the Beach would be perfect, but that one's taken. It seems like all the good cocktail names are taken: Bald Pussy, Cocksucking Cowboy, Sex on My Face. Maybe you could call this one Sex on the Kitchen Floor. It's been way too long since that happened. Never mind. Think of interesting questions for your book: How is a vodka bottle like a curling iron? What's the best direction to stir your drink: clockwise, counterclockwise, sideways figure eight? And most important, whose pants could you charm off?

Do some research on drinking writers. Jack Kerouac, at forty-seven, died of an internal hemorrhage caused by cirrhosis of the liver. Dylan Thomas, at thirty-nine, comatose after beers at the White Horse Tavern. Hemingway, who celebrated the running of the bulls and the slaughter of same, accompanied by good red wine from a goatskin, grew increasingly belligerent and paranoid and shot himself at sixty-one. Dorothy Parker, one of your favorites: usually drunk and often suicidal. Elizabeth Bishop was pretty happy with her girlfriend, Lota, down in their Brazilian paradise, but that didn't keep her from getting regularly sloshed. William Faulkner liked mint juleps; Hunter Thompson, Wild Turkey; Carson McCullers drank hot tea and sherry all day long, a mix she called "sonnie boy." Marguerite Duras had a tendency to binge and pass out. Jean Rhys, often poor and depressed, was a lifelong alcoholic. These were great writers. In "how to be a great writer," Charles Bukowski wrote, "beer is continuous blood./ a continuous lover."

Disbelieve the notion that writers drink more than other people because they are artists and unusually sensitive, whereas so-called normal people, those dullards, feel almost nothing at all. Then again, feel that you yourself are unusually sensitive. Socrates said the unexamined life is not worth living, but an article in the newspaper explained that people who seldom examine their lives are happier. Realize that most writers live overexamined lives.

In a poem, you once compared gin to a lover. After your

second marriage broke up, gin was your drink of choice. You felt kind of glamorous drinking it, weeping around your tiny apartment in the TV light, ordering the shit being touted in infomercials, wearing a long, flimsy white nightgown like a jilted creature out of Tennessee Williams. Williams, another major alcoholic. You don't drink gin anymore. You don't have a lover anymore, either. There isn't even a Gentleman Caller, not that he was exactly good news, dashing Laura's illusions, breaking her glass unicorn and fragile heart.

Try not to let your current lack of a love life be an excuse for getting drunker than a boiled owl. Wonder if you can be a great writer even though you rarely drink beer, even though *The New Yorker* just rejected those poems you sent that were your best ever. Screw *The New Yorker*. Delete their e-mail rejection and head to the liquor store up the street for a bottle of gin and one of Campari, then make a Negroni according to the recipe in the *Harry's Bar Cookbook* you bought in Venice after an obscenely expensive meal at Harry's with an ex-boyfriend. Remember the drunk you saw afterward, lurching in circles trying to make it to his hotel across the street. Remember how you loved that boyfriend. Remember that most of the poems in *The New Yorker*, let's be honest, suck.

MIMOSAS BECAUSE IT'S Sunday brunch. Cabernet sauvignon because it goes with the pizza. Sancerre because it's your favorite. House margarita, rocks, no salt, or else Patrón Silver with Cointreau and fresh lime juice, shaken and poured into a chilled martini glass. You drink because the dinner guests are boring and the conversation insipid. Because you're anxious about your upcoming travel. Because you're celebrating: a friend's birthday, a new book, the world not ending. Because you bought napkins that say, IT'S FIVE O'CLOCK SOMEWHERE. Because you like a glass of wine on the counter as you chop the garlic. Because your friend's sister's cough turned out to be cancer. Because your mother gets Parkinson's and spends a miserable ten years shuffling around in assisted living, and then dies. Because you are not with her when she does. Remember how fast she was on the tennis court, how she always jogged up stairs. Remember her enjoying a single bourbon and Coke almost every night with a bag of Fritos. The last time you played tennis with her was on a court near the retirement community in Florida where she stayed during the winters. Tall coconut palms beyond the chain-link fence, late afternoon light on their trunks and long fronds, your mother executing a series of perfect backhands. Afterward, you went out for drinks with your brother Gary. Remember giving vast quantities of whiskey to your brother Jon, when you and his girlfriend pierced his ear in high school.

Because Jon died less than a year after your mother, which made you understand in a more visceral way that everyone disappears. Because there is a feeling you want, and it isn't this one. Because a beer will help your hangover. Because you're falling in love with a man and are afraid to tell him. Because you're camping and the sun is going down over the river as you lie together on an old green blanket, in love, and when the wine spreads through you like melted blackberries, you will go into the tent and hold each other on top of the zipped-together sleeping bags. Remember saying, *"Please don't leave."* Because he left. Because fuck it. Because you're bored, restless, angry, disappointed, scared. Because who are you without it?

STOP SEEING YOUR friends who drink. This would be nearly all of them. One works in the wine business. You spent many happy evenings at his table while he brought up special bottles from his basement. Your friends are having parties, meeting at bars, going to readings where, afterward, there are receptions featuring horrifyingly bad wine and cheese cubes and crackers and cookies. Take your mind off all that; binge on episodes of *Scandal*, a TV series about a woman named Olivia Pope who fixes scandals in DC and has a torrid, tormented relationship with the leader of the free world. In nearly every episode, watch Olivia Pope drink red wine from big goblet-size glasses and sometimes straight from the bottle.

Grow depressed and isolated. Wonder if it's time to get back on Celexa. It has helped you in the past, when you've felt hopeless and wondered why we are born only to grow old and ill and die and be turned into a heavy plastic baggie of ash or have our faces eaten away by crawling things under the ground. This is how you think when you are depressed. Only other depressed people can understand how you feel, hunkered down on your own private promontory of despair, vultures circling above you, blotting out the wan sun. A lot of great writers, of course, were also depressed. This thought does not comfort you. Nothing can comfort you in this state, except maybe alcohol. She would be there for you constantly if only you didn't push her away sometimes and refuse to see her or even text her. She looks for you all over town. She's hanging out with all the people you have stopped calling, waiting for you to forgive her for whatever she's done. *Don't you love me anymore?* she says.

You are not supposed to drink while taking Celexa. When you were on it, you didn't drink nearly as much. Celexa took the edge off, the edge you have teetered on most of your life, falling in sometimes, climbing back out to the land of green energy drinks and regular exercise, determined to find your balance, to be someone in control of your habits and not enslaved by a capricious master who is often kind but who sometimes, for no apparent reason, attacks you with savage fury and leaves you broken, your head like a seawall pounded by a storm surge, a vague sense of guilt for you know not what hideous transgression. Call for an appointment with a sympathetic psychiatrist, and walk in looking as though you have lost your best friend.

RUN INTO THE orange traffic cones and keep driving. Steal spoons from one restaurant, candles from another. Drink and dial and sob into the phone. Go home with a man from the bar and give him a blow job. He's smart and interesting and witty and you think, *Maybe, finally.* He shows you the garden in back of his house and clips a rose for you. When you leave, you walk around to the driver's side of your car and he stays on the sidewalk. That's when he tells you that the woman he called his roommate isn't. She's his lover. He says, "You had a good time, right?" You throw the rose at him over the car roof, wishing it were a brick, then get in your car and drive away.

These are your memories. These are what you consist of, the lines on your palm that map your history and potential, the synapses in your brain flashing and buzzing like neon. Colored gas in a tube, so bright when lit, and then gray, dull when the plug is pulled. It's early morning. You're in someone's bed. The street outside looks ugly; the trash cans are pulled to the curb and overflowing. Where were you last night? Where are you now?

ONCE YOU WERE a child who knew her place in the world. It was a world brightened by Budweiser signs and pinball lights, a land with endless rivers of Shirley Temples carrying bushels of brightly dyed cherries. Your Skipper doll owned a pink coat with a matching umbrella, several flowered dresses, one-piece red-and-white-striped bloomers with a beribboned sun hat. She owned a skating outfit and a dirndl and a pony with a blue plastic saddle. You had undreamed-of wealth, though at the time it seemed but a handful of coins. Then you were exiled from that world forever. There is no going back. Not even a river of pure alcohol could take you there; not even writing can ferry you across. The river keeps carrying things away, and you remain planted beside it like a cottonwood, or a willow. This is where you belong now. Pay attention. Listen to what is passing.

Pants on Fire

As a writer occasionally tarred with the brush of being a "confessional poet," feathered with disdain and once even tied to a maypole by roving bands of critics, I'd like to reveal a few transgressions to you here and now. I hope you will forgive me. I can't seem to stop telling you everything about me in the lineated memoir of my life. This may be because I'm a woman, which means I am an emotional land mine waiting to be stepped on, a weeping, oversharing harpy whose inner weather fluctuates wildly. And women, as everyone knows, often lack that quality of imagination men have in such abundance.

In any case, I clearly have an inordinate, some might say excessive, need to kneel in a small dark space, separated from you by a little mesh screen, and reveal to you my impure thoughts and the number of times I dishonored my parents or coveted my neighbor's donkey. And now I must tell you how many times I have been guilty of lying my head off in my poems and of just plain making shit up. Although I hope you will see that I have also told the God's honest truth on occasion, because a writer must tell the truth at least some of the time, or who would ever want to listen to her bullshit?

I KILLED MY mother before she died. The poem was about death, and the conclusion was more satisfying if hers arrived suddenly in the last stanza, about ten years early. It's true the shapes of the clouds terrified me, but I did not smell "the bacon fat from breakfast," as the poem claims. I had seven-grain toast with blackberry preserves that day. I confess I feel ambivalent about bacon because pigs are intelligent animals, often cruelly treated on their way to slaughter and sometimes during the act itself. Yet I will not pass up roasted brussels sprouts if there happens to be a little bacon—or, better yet, prosciutto—wrapped around them after they have been steamed and then seared with oil in a pan with lots of garlic.

The dead friend in the poem was truly dead. I don't remember ever calling her and getting her answering machine, so I never heard her recorded voice say anything, let alone *"Hello I'm not here,"* but it is certainly true that she was not there in her apartment by the lake in Oakland. She had moved to her daughter's house in Sacramento to die, and that is where I saw her last and read poems to her while she drifted in a morphine haze.

As for the UPS man: the driver really did wear brown,

and I admit I found him attractive, especially when he wore shorts, but in the rigor of revision, I took that part out.

ANOTHER POEM CORRECTLY identified the woman making my cappuccino as a former girlfriend of the man I was seeing at the time. But I was the one who had his heart. After all, he brought me a sunflower he had stolen from a neighbor's yard. New love proved to be a boring subject, so in the interest of a good conflict, I wrote the poem as though I didn't know he was mine, or at least wasn't sure. In this way I managed to extend an idle thought as I waited for my cappuccino—*There's his ex*—into a lengthy meditation. Of course, eventually he would no longer be mine, so by that point the poem might as well have been true, and I would need to write several more poems about him, including one that described his private parts as accurately as my skills allowed. And his face, in all honesty, did close "like a failed business." I passed that place on my way to the bar and there he was, floating behind the dusty glass of the window. It is also true that as his former girlfriend handed me the change for my cappuccino, our fingers touched, but I don't remember what I was thinking about at that moment—certainly not the two of them. Maybe having to teach that graduate poetry class I hated.

I SWEAR ON a stack of Bibles that some men really will want "to fuck your poems."

MY HEART IS not "a Mississippi chicken shack." It is an organ, and I don't mean a Hammond B3. It's about the size of a fist, or a sopping wet tennis ball. Neither is my heart "a landing strip with no runway lights." I have heard of some women shaving their pubic hair in that manner, but I am not one of them. I happen to like pubic hair, and lots of it.

My mother played tennis extremely well. I miss her.

IT IS A big fat lie that the kitchen door in the house I grew up in "was kicked in to hang by a hinge." Nobody kicked it. My father and oldest brother fell into it while they were fighting, so it was clearly an accident and not at all intentional, as the poem falsely implies. Usually, when they fought, my other brothers and I stayed downstairs in the rec room smoking pot with our friends and laughing, unless we heard our mother getting involved, trying to separate the combatants, at which point a few boys would head upstairs to extricate her.

As for the babies I described floating in Limbo, their faces "stretched like balloons," how could I know what the hell they looked like? And I threw Satan in there even though I stopped believing in him when I was, like, seven.

That I hated my oldest brother "with a great purity of feeling" is another whopper. How can something pure make you feel so contaminated? Aren't we supposed to love one another? Does God hate us—is that why He allows evil to exist?

———

THERE WAS AN actual tsunami on December 26, 2004. According to Wikipedia, the earthquake that caused it lasted nearly ten minutes, and more than 230,000 people died. The planet vibrated. Just as I wrote, souls were arriving and departing, though the departure gate was clearly more crowded. I made up the Akashic angel whose job it is to write everything down, pausing for an instant and then furiously scribbling, detailing names and faces, memories and unfulfilled dreams, keeping track. No one keeps track except us.

ALL THAT YEAR my friend wanted to kill herself. She would call me late at night, drunk and sobbing, talking about her gun. Finally I convinced her to throw it into the river. Eventually she got much better, but I still worried about her. I thought of her as the little bullet-size ballerina on my jewelry box, spinning and slowing, then spinning again. That she gave me the box was a complete fabrication. She did not give me the box. What she gave me was a picture book called *Six-Dinner Sid*, about a cat that goes from door to door getting fed by everyone on the block, and another one about a farting dog at a garage sale, and once, to celebrate the publication of my first novel, she gave me a plastic baby bottle with a blue ribbon on it. The truth is that she's much better now. The truth is also that I still worry.

———

It is possible to feel "happiness after grief," just as I wrote, though when I saw my neighbor's two-year-old granddaughter running around naked except for a fox stole, I wasn't grieving. I may have been a little depressed. Then again, I may have been merely bored and slightly anxious, sitting at my desk and staring out the window hoping something poetic would happen out there so I could write it down, go play with my cat, and pick up some taco fixings for dinner with my boyfriend.

I confess to happiness; that's no jive. Especially since I got back on Celexa, I no longer feel that the world is a darkling plain, swept with confused alarms of failed romances and *Fuck-you*s. I confess to grief, to death like a stone well, loved ones falling in, never to surface again. I confess that a kelson of my creations is love. The poems are not the life. "Liar, liar, pants on fire, nose as long as a telephone wire," the little girls outside my window are singing, skipping rope, and, singing, into my litany they go.

Flu Shot

FIRST I HAVE to convince my mother to go. She has some-how missed the scheduled on-site flu shots, and my brother Gary has asked me to take her over to the drugstore. I'm sitting in her ugly room at Summerville Assisted Living in Potomac, Maryland. Why don't they ever name these places truthfully? They aren't fooling anyone. Sunrise Villa, Tranquility Manor, Renaissance Gardens, Spring Meadows. I'd like to see End of the Road, or Senior Warehouse Outlet. Summerville should properly be called Soon Dead of Winter.

"Come on, Mom, up and at 'em," I say, inanely. *Up and at 'em?* Where did that come from? *Let's go tackle that flu shot right now.* She can barely bring herself to lift her head. She lies in her bed, looking at the wall.

"Wait," she says.

"The sooner we go, the sooner we can come back."

"Huh," she says.

On the wall of her room is a painting: my mother as a young woman, wielding a tennis racket like a rapier, lunging for a low backhand. Her famous backhand. My famous mother. Wimbledon Singles champion in 1946, four times US Open champion. The artist has painted her on a path in a forest. Is she supposed to be aiming for a tennis ball that has landed in the light-dappled duff, or about to bash in the head of some forest creature? The painting is dumb, the room sterile. A few broken shelves hold books whose type she can't quite see. I've bought her every kind of magnifying device I could find, but she's grown too confused to use any of them. There are some leftovers from her once-extensive collection of miniature pianos. She used to collect clowns, too, but those have disappeared, along with the windup statuette of Elvis at the piano that played "How Great Thou Art." A basket of Oreos languishes on the table beside a bouquet of exhausted flowers in greenish water. The curtains, made of some white plastic material, are always closed. Sometimes I have to go to the window and peek out there, just to make sure the world hasn't been replaced by blankness, that there really is a place where trees sprout new leaves and birds sit on the branches. Though, as soon as I have done this, I immediately think, *"Bare ruined choirs, where late the sweet birds sang."*

My mother used to sit and read in the library down the hall or walk around and around the garden courtyard for exercise. She also used to sneak out and make a dangerous crossing to the shopping center across the street, I suspect hoping to be hit by a car. But now she is mostly confined to her room, too weak for much of anything else.

Eventually, if she lives long enough, she'll have to go Upstairs. Upstairs is the third floor of Summerville, a place my mother knows of and fears. It's where people go when they can't cut it any longer with the level of care they are getting on the first two floors. The first two floors are bad enough: wheelchaired stroke victims and vacant-eyed residents slumped in matching chairs. She's depressed about being here. Who wouldn't be? I walk into Summerville and no matter what my mood, it instantly drops about thirty degrees. Summerville makes me think of what Denis Johnson wrote in his short story "Beverly Home," after describing the residents: *They made God look like a senseless maniac.*

"Wait, wait," my mother says. She doesn't want to go get a flu shot. She wants to sleep. There is no way to move her if she doesn't want to go.

I came from California for this visit, planning to get a few things done. In previous visits, I accomplished the Clipping of the Toenails and the Buying of the Shower Mat, tasks that on my private scale of difficulty fell somewhere between challenging and overwhelming. My tendency is to hide from the mundane tasks of the world, to prefer imagination to reality; this is one reason I became a writer. Most of the year, Gary does the truly hard work with our mother. He visits her daily, takes care of the bills, the doctor visits, the complex negotiations with various infernal bureaucracies.

Yesterday I managed the Cleaning of the Dentures, prying them out of her mouth, plopping them into a glass with an Efferdent tablet to fizz away bacteria, applying the powder meant to help the dentures grip the gums. I used to stare at my grandmother's teeth, which spent their nights in a glass of water in a bathroom of our old house, and now I found myself staring at my mother's teeth, this part of her body that I had dislodged. I wanted to get them back in as quickly as possible. I never imagined her old like this—my slim, athletic mother. But now it's hard to imagine her any other way: her stoop-shouldered walk, her stained clothing, her closed eyes as she lies in bed waiting for her daughter to return her teeth.

Her eyes are closed again. "Mom?" I say.

She's sleeping, or pretending to. I reflect on the good luck of having nearly all my teeth. I play weekly tennis with a friend, do yoga and weights at the gym. I'm taking the poet's advice: "*Do not go gentle into that good night.*" I have become a poet myself, have racked up a few of my own victories, books and grants and prizes. If my luck holds, no one will ever paint me writing on my laptop in a forest. The overhead smash of Parkinson's won't blindside me, as it did my mother.

I think about opening her curtains, now that she is sleeping, but I can't seem to get up the energy to get out of the leather swivel chair by her bed.

After half an hour she wakes up. Her head turns, her eyes open, and she blinks, surprised to see me.

"Mom," I say. "You need to get up. We have to get you a flu shot. And listen, while we're there, I'll buy you some Cheez-Its."

My mother has developed an unholy love for Cheez-Its. If she doesn't have at least a couple of boxes, she gets that look in her eye, the look of an addict down to the last of the heroin, filled with anxiety that there won't be a wake-up shot for the next morning. Once, there were sports columnists following her every move, and visits to the Riviera with her friend Barbara Hutton, the Woolworth heiress once married to Cary Grant. There were doubles matches with Groucho Marx as her partner. (She took so many of the balls that came their way that he left the court and came back with a sleeping bag and unrolled it in the service box.) My mother dated Jack Dempsey. She had a fling with Spencer Tracy during one of his breaks from Katharine Hepburn. He gave her a gold bracelet that read, TO THE CHAMP FROM SILVER-TOP. My brothers and I used to look at it and fantasize that Spencer Tracy was our real father, not because we didn't like our actual father but because we were seduced by the idea that famous people were better than us. For my mother, who by the time she was my mother was only a formerly famous person, there had been the Wimbledon and US Open championships and the finals of the French Open, the Wightman Cup team, exhibition matches, and newspaper photos. There had been golf and jogging and swimming. When she took me to London in the eighties for an event honoring the female Wimbledon champions, we ate strawberries and clotted cream with the Duke and Duchess of Kent. There were daily rides to the tournament in the special green Wimbledon minicars, and chats with Martina Navratilova. Now there is Summerville, and fumbling at the buttons on her sweater. Now there are Cheez-Its.

"We'll get three boxes," I say. Never mind that there are a couple of boxes here already. It is impossible to be oversupplied.

"Oh," she says. "Okay."

Trembling, she manages to sit up, with me supporting her. Luckily she is already dressed. If I had to dress her, too, I'd likely just give up on the idea of the flu shot and sink back into my chair while she sank back into her bed. But she's dressed, in a stained blouse and sweatpants, and I've told Gary I will do this one small thing before I go back to California to feel guilty that my mother needs me and I am not there.

I get her into a coat, afraid of breaking her thin arm as I guide it toward the sleeve. Does she know what's going on? At times it's hard to tell. She has some dementia. And my mother rarely disclosed her feelings, so now it is very hard to tell.

Come to think of it, the only one in our family who freely expressed himself was my oldest brother, though mostly his feelings were "Fuck you" and "I hate you." He had no problem screaming or trashing the furnishings, chasing his siblings around the dining room table with a kitchen knife, stabbing his mother with scissors. He threw punches at our father once he got big enough to have a shot at doing some damage. There were five of us kids—four boys and me, along with a nanny for several years, plus my grandmother. Our father was nice enough (toward most of us, anyway), but as a sportswriter he traveled a lot, and when he was at home he rose after we went to school and came home after we were asleep. We saw him mostly on weekends, mowing the lawn or sitting with his back to us at MacDonald's Raw Bar. Our mother pretty much lived on a tennis court, the way some mothers live in the kitchen whipping up meals and desserts. Our big split-level house was like a vast African savanna where we roamed around hunting for food, staying out of our oldest brother's way, occasionally having savage encounters.

I don't recall my mother ever approaching me to hug me. What I remember is that at some point I started hugging her, telling her I loved her, and that she then said, "I love you, too." Probably, though, my memory is faulty and has lied. And my mother wasn't cold. She was kind to everyone, and witty, and as her only daughter I felt we had a special bond. But she was also private and, I've come to believe, damaged early in some way that led her to withdraw from us, to focus her life on tennis. She fell in love with a sport, gave it everything, and it loved her back for most of her life.

She manages to stand, and we push her walker down the hall. It says CHAMP in Magic Marker on a piece of masking tape on the front. We leave it in the lobby, since it won't fit into my rental car, and besides, she wants to walk to the car on her own. I hold her hand, ready to lunge to keep her from the ground. Hours, lifetimes pass just getting her into the car. She bends down to the open door. Surely she'll fall now. She's fallen often this past year, getting bruised and banged up, once landing in the hospital with a femoral fracture. I keep my hand near the top of the window frame so she won't hit her head. Then she's in. She doesn't sit back in the seat; it's more like she contorts into its general area. I wrestle the seat belt around her.

The street in front of Summerville has surprisingly heavy traffic. It takes a while just to pull out of the driveway. When I get to the shopping center, there isn't anywhere to park near the drugstore, and I'm not sure what to do. I can't just leave her at the curb while I find a space. She'll fall, or wander off. So I circle the parking lot, which properly should be called the Aquarium, the Fish Tank of Mortal Life, all of us circling and dying, circling and breathing and still moving. At last there's a space close to the store, and I take it.

"I can do it," she says when I try to help her from the car. Bracing her hands on the seat, she tries to rise, putting in a mighty effort, giving it her feeble all, and nothing happens. I reach for her but "I can do it, I can do it"—this is my mother after all, the tennis champion with the killer instinct, cover of *Time* magazine, September 2, 1946. Underneath a color illustration of her face superimposed on the head of a tennis racket, it read, CALIFORNIA'S PAULINE BETZ. THE SPICE OF HER LIFE: COMPETITION. The price then was twenty cents. The racket was wood; her hair was blonde. The article described her as "a friendly, attractive and aggressive American girl" with "a terrifying determination not to lose at anything."

I stand, waiting, and finally, miraculously, she does it; she rises from the car. I take her arm and steer us across the parking lot. How long before she collapses—two more steps, five? I can see she's flagging badly, and we're only to the curb. There is still the wide sidewalk to get across, the store to enter, and the pharmacy is in the rear of the store. But it's too late to turn back. We are on an expedition.

Inside the store, I lead her toward the Minute Clinic, the destination, the grail of the flu vaccine that will keep her from dying of influenza this winter, that will keep her alive. *For what?* I think. And then, *What is wrong with me?* I pray that she doesn't need an appointment, that we haven't made this journey for nothing.

Another woman stands at the computer by the clinic, signing in. My mother collapses into a chair and takes on the look of an abandoned pile of dirty laundry. The passing shoppers are probably wondering whom that poor old woman belongs to. I have the urge to walk away from her. How long would she sit there before somebody grew concerned? There is definitely something wrong with me. She wasn't a bad mother, just a flawed one. Who can say of their parents, "They were perfect; they didn't damage me in any way"? No one I would count among my friends.

When it's finally her turn, I hoist her from the chair and take her into the small room where they give the shots. I try to unzip her coat, but the zipper is stuck at the bottom, separated; no matter how I tug and fiddle with it, I can't undo it. The Minute Clinic clinician—call her the Angel of Mercy— suggests pulling the coat off the shoulder and unbuttoning my mother's blouse to bare her arm for the shot. Does she feel humiliated, my mother who smells bad, who wears no bra, as the nice woman unbuttons her drool-encrusted blouse? No matter, I feel humiliated for her. She gets the shot.

I hand over my Visa, take some paperwork, and guide her back to the car. I turn back into the same heavy traffic, go through two lights, and then there is a left turn into the facility (which should properly be called "the difficulty"). It takes several minutes to make the turn, all the cars schooling toward me, no one giving an inch, everyone getting somewhere. At last there's an opening I can shoot through so I can pull the car up, get her out of it, and sit her down in the lobby again while I park.

"Which way is my room?" she says, at the intersection of two hallways. "*Two roads diverged in a yellow wood*," I think. It didn't ultimately matter which one you took; that was the real point of Frost's poem. The roads were pretty much the same. That stuff about the one less traveled making all the difference was bullshit.

At last we are safely back in the company of the TV, the tacky art, the tiny silent pianos. My mother used to have a white baby grand in her condo. When I was young she would sit at her old upright banging out some popular song from the forties, like "Some Enchanted Evening" or "Don't Get Around Much Anymore." I don't feel like I ever really knew her, knew what she felt about her life before us kids, and after us. Mostly, growing up, I saw her on the other side of a tennis net, the regulation court marking off the distance between us.

But probably, again, that is a lie—the kind memory tells when trying to make sense of the story. If I allow for a messier story, I also remember us as close. I remember her singing Irish lullabies to me at bedtime, reading me fairy tales, hitting tennis balls to me and saying "Good, good," no matter what I did. "Good" when I hit the ball into the fence, when I missed the ball entirely. I remember sitting on the lid of the toilet to keep her company while she took her evening bath, her breasts floating in the water, her legs tanned, her ankles and feet white from her tennis shoes and socks. Our fights would inevitably end with one of us making an ironic, deadpan remark, and then we would be laughing together. When I was in high school, we collaborated on stories for the school paper, and for years afterward one of us would mention Johnny Necro—the dead boy we invented to illustrate the problem of being sick (or dead) and not being able to go to the school nurse without a pass—and we would crack up. I remember how proud of me she was, even when she didn't quite understand what I was up to. "It's nice you have your poetry, the way I have bridge," she used to say. For years, when I told her I was traveling somewhere to give a reading, she would say, skeptically, "They pay you for that?" Yes, Mom, they pay me. Usually.

While we were at the shopping center, someone has come in and pulled back the covers on the bed. There's a large pad in the middle of the bed in case my mother's adult diaper leaks. I sit her down and again try to get the damned fucking zipper unzipped. The metal teeth line up. I take off the coat and help her lie down and cover her with a sheet. She looks like she's been through a trauma, and I suppose she has.

I stroke her hair. My heart feels wrung out. I lay my palm against her cheek and tell her I love her. I can't wait to get back to Gary's house and pour a big glass of wine. I say good-bye, but she looks as though she has already fallen asleep.

As my mother declines further, over the next months and years, I begin to pay particular attention to the old. There aren't many to be seen where I live in Oakland. They aren't in the bars or restaurants or music venues. Occasionally, not far from the senior housing complex, I see them shuffling glacially through a crosswalk, pushing their walkers to the grocery store. Their hands shake as they pull items from their cart. They take forever to count out their wrinkled dollar bills and hand them over to the cashier. I used to be impatient, caught in line behind them. Now I try to catch their eye, to let them know I know: it's true, God is a senseless maniac. And they are champions.

All Manner of Obscene Things

I GO INTO the kitchen to take a couple of hits off a joint by the open window, blowing the smoke into the salt-scented air. It's where my boyfriend often stands because it's the only place in the house I'll let him smoke his Camel Lights. It's also the place where you can see the Pacific Ocean, down the hill less than a mile away. I wave the smoke toward the ocean and hurry back to our bedroom before my teenage daughter can come out of hers and catch me.

I've been watching TV for five minutes when Aya walks into my bedroom and says, "Mom, are you stoned?"

"No," I say, but she can tell. "So?" I say.

She shrugs and walks out. I'm always doing something wrong. The latest wrong thing is cheating on my boyfriend with my second ex-husband, whom Aya justifiably hates. When they first met, she didn't like him much. She already had a father, my first ex-husband, and didn't see the need of a second one hanging around us. Then he won her over. I have a picture to prove it, from a day we visited my father's grave. My second husband leans against the car door, his arm around Aya as she leans into him, a tiny eight-year-old with a blaze of blonde hair. I have another photo from that day, too, that he took without my knowing it. I'm on my knees beside the grave and a jar of wildflowers. Aya is hugging me, her face against my shoulder.

Then he left us, and I did a lot of crying and drinking. Aya loves my current boyfriend, and so do I, but I'm leaving him. I've been looking for an apartment. I can't afford anything as nice as this house we've been renting, with its high ceilings and cheerful orange walls. When Aya was in junior high, she and I shared a one-bedroom apartment; she had the bedroom, and I had a futon in the living room. Now that she's in high school we're going to need something bigger, but all the places in my price range are small and ugly.

We meet on Mondays, the ex-husband and I. We hold each other's hand in restaurants and can't let go. We kiss in his car at Stop signs until another car comes up and the driver leans hard on his horn. We make love in his van, and in his flat, on the couch that smells faintly of the mice that live in it. I am too much in love to fully register the mice. By the time I do, we will be moving together to a small house in Oakland. Eventually he will borrow a large sum of money from me without my knowing it, and when I find out, that will be that. But for now, we are soul mates. We believe in our love as fervently as crazed zealots believe that by standing on an overturned crate and screaming at a busy intersection, they are bringing the word of God to the infidels.

I am deliriously happy, and I am hurting everyone.

EVERY CHILD IS born with a tiny part of its imagination missing, the part that can visualize Mommy and Daddy, or Mommy and Mommy, or Daddy and Daddy, naked and sweating together as all manner of obscene things occur. When I first learned about the man putting his penis in the woman, it never occurred to me that this abstract knowledge could be applied to my parents. Even once accidentally seeing my father's penis, when he emerged naked from my parents' bathroom, didn't convince me he was capable of having an erection, let alone placing that thing in my mother's vagina. Even writing these words, I feel faintly horrified.

I have seen my mother's vagina. I washed it a few times, toward the end of her life. Still, I could not imagine my father making love with her. And it's only now, after her death, that I can even think of her as a woman who was once a sexual crea-ture, who must have slept with some of those early boyfriends she reminisced about in the years after my father died. Once, I asked her about her affair with Spencer Tracy. When she was a tennis star, my mother knew all sorts of famous people.

"Did you sleep with him?" I asked. She was visiting me in San Francisco. We were sitting on the beach at the Marina, our shoes off, our bare feet in the cool sand.

"Oh, Spence was a lot of fun," she said, with a sly little smile, and I didn't press her for details.

So I figure Aya could have done without knowing that her mother was off having sex with Fuckface, as we'd once nicknamed the ex-husband, messing up our life with a good boyfriend and a nice house with walls painted a color called Mango Tango and a view of the ocean, as well as her basement bedroom, where she could sneak her own boyfriend in and out without anyone knowing. And this was only the latest wrong thing. Before this, there had been that piece of pornography I published in *Penthouse*. Aya wasn't supposed to see it, but my boyfriend pulled it off its hiding place on top of the fridge and said, "Look! Your mom's in *Penthouse*." At least I wasn't in there spread over a hay bale with my airbrushed anus shining, but still. No teenager wants to hear, "Your mom is in *Penthouse*." I wasn't on the cover of *Time*, like my own mom had been; I was in a dirty magazine read under the covers and out in the woods by preadolescents. Somewhere, grown men were masturbating thanks to my words. I had written the story with a list of guidelines like "no bestiality" and "no excessive cum on the face."

This is the kind of mother I was.

I'M SORRY I broke your Easy-Bake Oven the first time we used it, the little tray melted and mangled, the giant cookie burned beyond recognition. I'm sorry I accidentally sewed the cutout pieces of your purple tuxedo for the preschool concert to the bed covers and threw that metronome at your father's head during an argument in the kitchen while you cowered in the hall, three years old and crying. Sorry I brought those guys home from the bar while you were sleeping, so you had to come out to the living room when we woke you playing music and worry I'd be raped. I'm sorry I got so drunk at the restaurant that I ate the napkin with the playwright's phone number on it and kissed another woman in front of all your friends. I know there's a lot more. I love you more than you will ever understand, unless you have a child of your own, and even then it will take years, as it did with my own mother. Two years after her death, our relationship continues, and I am still trying to understand.

MY BOYFRIEND IN the house with the view of the ocean was sweet and terribly good-looking, and every woman we met flirted madly with him. He cheated on me only once, with a bar girl in Bangkok, on a business trip. He was out with a bunch of his business associates. They were all drinking heavily, and I guess you can imagine the rest. He came home and told me right away. I wrote an angry short story about it, and then I forgave him.

Of the boyfriends and husbands, he was my mother's favorite. Somewhere I have a movie of the two of them dancing in Las Vegas. My mother and aunt were there to play a bridge tournament, and one night the bridge players had a party. The room was full of old people in hideous outfits, talking obsessively about the hands they'd been dealt that afternoon. My mother wore a sweater appliquéd with shiny playing cards; my aunt had on a sequined sweatshirt. When the DJ put on Frank Sinatra—"Strangers in the night, exchanging glances"—my boyfriend asked my mother to dance, and all the old women, I imagine, sighed at the sight of a young, handsome man with longish hair and one earring spinning my mother around the floor. My mother loved to dance. For years afterward, when I visited her in her condo and then in assisted living, she would say, "How's my favorite beau?" I would tell her he was fine, though I didn't know. A friend got a note from him after we broke up, saying he'd gotten married—it was really my friend who received the note, not his, so I'm pretty sure he just wanted me to know. "I met my soul mate!" was what he wrote, but I understood the secret message: "Fuck off and die, Kim, I'm over you."

I took the movie of my mother and boyfriend dancing with a new video camera I'd bought thanks to a grant from the National Endowment for the Arts. The other movies I have are of a different sort. They are marked PRIVATE and XXX. In the one we shot in our Vegas hotel room with the aid of a tripod, I'm a casino waitress in a short skirt, bringing him drinks, and he tips me a twenty each time. I also play the dealer, sitting down topless to flip cards faceup on the hotel desk in front of him. He's a pipe salesman from Des Moines who's losing, but he's a gambling addict, so he just keeps placing more bad bets until all the poker chips are on my side of the desk. Guess how he gets more chips? For a while we made movies with all the passion of the Mitchell Brothers, the famous San Francisco porn kings who opened the O'Farrell Theatre in the Tenderloin district. Then we got used to our new toy, and each other, and settled down into a more normal sex life, with only occasional blindfolds and cross-dressing and visits to Good Vibrations for toys we sometimes had to get phone help to figure out.

I will probably never watch those movies again, but I can't bring myself to throw them away. In them I am younger and mostly naked, except for a sexy costume or two. My boyfriend looks like a cross between a young Paul Newman and a Roman god. Loud music is pulsing, and we are doing obscene things that aren't obscene because we are in love, laughing at how cheesy we are being, then forgetting all about the camera watching us. After this we will leave the hotel room, or the bedroom. We'll eat Chinese buffet with my mother and aunt, or make dinner together in our kitchen, or barbecue on the deck downstairs with a few friends. We'll part three years later, with tears and anger, and I'll never see him again.

Aya can never see those movies. Even writing this, imagining her reading these words, I am faintly horrified.

PARENTS COME TO know this about raising children to adulthood: you do the best you can for them, make unimaginable sacrifices, and then they leave you. They separate, as therapists say. What this means is that your heart now has a permanent hole in it. The child who once clung to your legs when you tried to leave the room, who sang made-up songs while arranging apples in intricate patterns on the living room rug, who begged to sleep in your bed and had to be sent sternly back to her own—that child is gone forever. In her place is a sensitive, talented, lovely young woman you have to keep from staring at when you are with her, she is so beautiful.

AYA AND I are having breakfast together under some tall skinny palm trees, the kind I remember from spending winters in Florida as a child. These are Southern California palms, with browning fronds that rattle in the occasional breeze. I'm visiting Aya to see the play she's in. Her character is a young woman who's cheating on her husband. We're miles and years away from my own drama, from the house and the boyfriend and ex-husband; they're tiny figures in the lens of memory, getting lost the way so much in life gets lost. One day they'll be nearly invisible, unless I write about them, but even so, it's hard to keep them in focus. I'm eating the most delicious almond croissant, and the air smells like jasmine. Purple jacaranda blossoms are swirling down from the trees. My daughter is with me. Tonight I'm staying at her rented studio, and we'll go to sleep in the same bed. I'll stay awake a little longer to watch her.

She's been married for a year. She wants to have a baby, but she's not ready yet; she's focused on her acting career. For a while she was getting a string of small, similar roles in film and TV: junkie girlfriend, New York prostitute, Russian prostitute. Then she got the lead in a play titled *Whore*.

"You know what," I tell her over breakfast, feeling it's time to broach the subject, "when we lived with that boyfriend there were some, ah, um, movies he and I made together of, you know, a sexual nature. I'm writing an essay . . ." My voice trails off. What was I thinking? I can never publish the essay. I want to take my words out of the flower-scented air, weight them with chains, and throw them in the ocean. Some things are better left unsaid.

"You mean those porn videos?" she says cheerfully. "I knew about those."

Now I am truly horrified. "You did?"

"You had that locked closet, remember? Come on. Teenager? Locked room? We picked the lock."

"You—"

"My friends and I started to watch one, but, *eww*, we turned it off when we realized. Wow, I'd totally forgotten about that until you brought it up. That boyfriend was nice, but some of the things in that room—"

"Okay, never mind," I tell her. The breeze blows a few blossoms onto our picnic table. The fronds rattle overhead. *Oh God oh God*, I'm thinking.

"I had secrets, too, you know," Aya says.

"Let's talk about something else," I say. My own mother was a master of deflection. If I tried to talk to her about some Deep Important Feeling I was having, she'd ask if I had any good writing students. She'd ask about her favorite beau. Her eyes would go to the TV, where people on some talk show were baring their souls to a studio audience.

Before this play, Aya had a handful of minutes of screen time in a Scorsese movie. In one scene, her line is something like "Make an appointment if you want to see him." In two other brief scenes, she utters these lines, respectively: "Lick my twat" and "Go fuck your cousin."

Over breakfast, she tells me she improvised those last two.

"Oh, honey, I'm so proud of you," I say, and we laugh, mother and daughter sharing a moment.

Not Dancing

In the middle of the day I was eating huge handfuls of baked four-cheese crisps and drinking diet root beer, wondering if I should just open some wine. Why not? I was alone and feeling slightly crazy; a glass of wine would be good company. But I have always felt that drinking alcohol before 5:00 p.m. is like watching TV during the day: loser behavior. And I was a winner, lying on a couch in a sunroom while it poured rain outside, rain on the skylight, rain on the big thirsty trees, on the blue table umbrella, the table and chairs and the brick patio being slowly devoured by weeds. I had several entire days to do whatever I wanted. What I wanted was to write; I'd organized my schedule around creating this time, a week of space and privacy in this farmhouse. But just like someone on unemployment who has given up looking for work as the benefits are running out, I had given up trying to write as the precious days, gray and sodden, trickled away. Summer, upstate New York: continual rain, cheese crisps, and writer's block.

Freewriting is the most common prescription for writer's block. Liberate yourself! Write anything at all, and cast out that judgy little hobgoblin on your shoulder. What matters is that you get something down. Poet William Stafford offered the advice that writers who feel stuck should simply lower their standards. But this, for me, is like saying, *If you're tired of being alone, just go ahead and invite the homeless guy who admired your cowboy boots back to your apartment. He'd be happy to solve your loneliness problem.* But we all know how that works. I'm not convinced that freewriting is actually *writing*, just as walking across a room is not dancing. And for the record, sex is not making love, though I have often been confused, myself, on this point. Poetry is not one of your latest freewrites broken up into lines and scattered over the page. What you've got there, honey, is some crap you wrote, nothing more or less. Sometimes we're just chimpanzees typing "banana banana banana," and it will never become "Now is the winter of our discontent made glorious summer . . ." Go ahead, keep a journal and put down everything that happens to you; it's probably not going to turn into real writing, unless your name is Anaïs Nin or Sylvia Plath.

I realize I'm going against the grain here. I've never read *The Artist's Way*, but I hear the author recommends something called Morning Pages. Well, if it works for her, or anyone, more power to them. My Morning Pages, if I wrote them, would still say, "Banana banana banana," nine times out of ten.

It's that tenth one, I suppose, you get lucky on. But I've always been a quitter. I can handle about three days of freewriting garbage, and then I give up and feel hopeless.

Which is what happened in the farmhouse. During the first three days, I typed a few tepid, inert statements and many clichés. My mind, at times a speakeasy teeming with fascinating ideas, now had been raided by the vice squad. The party-goers had all fled. The stale smell of dead cigarettes infected the curtains.

I looked through some failed pieces of writing, combing through the rubble for any signs of life, but all was eerily silent. I read a book of poems about a love affair, hoping to trigger anything: a rhythm, a subject, a stray memory that might suddenly come to light. I needed inspiration. Soon I felt inspired to consider my loneliness. I turned to nonfiction and read pieces about dwarfs, Mexican storytellers, and prison meals, hoping a suitable essay topic would occur to me. I tried to think of what interesting things had happened lately. Let's see: The bathroom here appeared to have a small leak. I found the Wi-Fi café in town, and got lost going to the grocery store. There were three little chicks out there in the birdhouse in the yard, cozy in their nest. Life, friends, was boring. I had absolutely nothing to say.

I wish I could tell you that the next day I had a recovered memory of Satanic ritual abuse or went into town and witnessed something dramatic: a quarrel, then a stabbing, the victim falling backward, clutching the blooming wound in his chest, toppling into a bunch of orange tiger lilies. Or even that a chick made its way out of the round opening in its little house and plummeted into the soaked grass, that I carried it tenderly into the house and wrapped it in a dish towel and fed it with an eyedropper. That in each case I raced to my laptop and began to write, having at last found some subject matter to explore.

But nothing happened. It rained some more. I watched twelve DVDs. I went to town for the Wi-Fi and read Facebook posts, and for the zillionth time I wondered why I'd ever wanted to become a writer. The truth is that writing is simply not reliable. You can't count on it to be there just because you've made some space for it. In fact, making space might make it disappear. You tell yourself you can't write in the middle of your daily life, with all its distractions and commitments, and when you finally clear the decks, light off for someplace scenic or at least private, you sit there completely paralyzed. You have devoted yourself to writing, but it has not returned your devotion. If writing were a person, you would be in an abusive relationship. The healthy thing to do would be to get a restraining order and shut it right out of your heart.

Another day passed, and another. I tried to think of some suitable figurative language for "*Another day passed.*" Another day slunk away into the dark woods and howled. Another day shook a slimy brown banana peel in my face, bared its teeth, and went to splash in the growing puddle in the driveway. The bathroom leak got a little bigger; water dripped steadily down into the kitchen. My time to write, like my time on earth, was running out. Though I had published books, though I had written many poems and stories and essays and even two novels, the truth now appeared in all its stark clarity: I would never write again. Writing had deserted me. I should say good riddance, but I was hopelessly in love with the bastard.

Many people think that writers of published books never suffer this kind of difficulty. But virtually every writer I know has gone through long dry spells, through periods of not being able to face the work before them—or even having a clue about what that work might be. When we talk about the writing life, we don't just mean getting words on the page; we also mean those times we desperately want to write, but can't. It helps to know that many fine and even great writers experienced this dark night of the soul, and eventually came out the other side. Franz Kafka's diaries are filled with anguished lines about his inability to find the Muse. *The end of writing. When will it take me up again?* one entry reads. Another puts it even more succinctly: *Complete standstill. Unending torments.* And here's Virginia Woolf in her diary: *I am overwhelmed with things I ought to have written about and never found the words.* Yet these writers knew to keep at it, even if there were many bad days, even if they had to take a break now and then to let inspiration edge closer.

On my last evening upstate, having polished off another box of cheese crisps and started in on a bag of cheddar Goldfish, I opened some wine. Wine was reliable. It cared about me deeply and listened sympathetically as I got drunk to the point of crying and muttering about my many failings, all of which it instantly forgave me for. I crawled into bed with a novel and was soon lost in a story about a remote cliffside village in Italy. At least I could still read. At least there were still books, though from this point on they would not be written by me.

When I was sleepy, I put the novel aside and rolled over. A tiny laugh came from beneath me. It had emerged from the little stuffed animal I travel with. It's about the size of my hand and has a giant head with enormous eyes, white fur, stunted thalidomide limbs, a pink-and-gray-striped tail. I think it's supposed to be a lemur. It has a voice box, but it hadn't laughed for months. I'd figured the thing had worn out, run down, whatever. I pulled my little lemur from beneath me and gave it a squeeze, but now it just looked at me with its Keane eyes, those huge, cheesy, roundly glittering fakes.

But still, I thought. *I heard you laugh.*

How I Write

I WRITE BY osmosis. I write by divine decree. I write by heart, the heart shaking itself off like a dog that has nearly drowned in light. Or the heart dimly lit, sputtering and darkening, the heart shattering and held together again with duct tape and kindergarten paste. I write by memory, which is a beautiful liar. I write lies. I write in a secret universe, in bed, hating the world and the word *I*. I write at a desk and feel virtuous. I write without a thought in my head. I write groveling for love and attention, and also indifferent to everyone and everything. I write crap, shit, clichés, whiny complaints, black speculations, goofy formulations, and give up. I go back and write, "nada nada nada I suck why can't I write anything," and give up again. I write something I like, and the next day I realize it's shit. I write a poem, a story, a novel, an essay, a play. Each time, I'm lost. Each time, I wish

I hadn't started down this road, where I can't see my hand in front of my face, a ravine on my right, a swamp on my left; there's no one else walking where I'm walking, sometimes I'm crawling, sometimes I stop and cry. Then there are stars, or a cloud shreds itself before the moon, and I get up and keep walking. Sometimes I run and there is no pleasure like running down this road in the near dark, the wind full of voices, the air alive and fluid. I write and it's finally right, the intention rhyming with the result, the marvelous unforeseen surprise of a field flowering with kisses. I write and it's good and I am queen of the kingdom and every flower is for me. I write and it's not good enough; I go and read someone who is very, very good, and feel inspired, and go back and write again. Or feel so discouraged I give up for that day, for a week, for nearly a month, until I stop believing the kingdom exists. I am cursed, until one day, mysteriously, the curse lifts. I go back to writing over and over, the irresistible lover I have known for most of my life, the monster that controls me, the jabbering creature on my back, the mother who wounds me with grace. I persist. There is a road that doesn't end until I end, and then there is another road, and another I, trying again to tell you something true.

Simple Christian
Charity

THE SUBJECT HEADING of the e-mail in my in-box is just
my oldest brother's name. In the instant before I open the
e-mail, I anticipate what it will say: *"I'm sorry to be writing
you with the news that your brother died tragically . . ."* I imagine the possibilities: accident, illness, or, possibly—in fact,
likely—suicide. I also anticipate my feelings, in the following order: Relief. A flicker of loss, and then whatever the
emotional equivalent of a shrug might be. Shit happens.
Whatever. He's dead. Good riddance.

What the e-mail actually says is this:

Hi Kim,
I went to school with your brother. I have
been talking with him once a month or so.
He has lost almost everything and is trying

to get some government benefits. He has had
some teeth pulled because he cannot afford
to have implants. He is depressed over his
new predicament. He has moved to _____.
I am including his phone number. Please
give him a short call. I think it would mean
a lot to him.

Thank you.

Sincerely,
Walter Morris

My feelings now occur in this order: Disappointment. A flicker of sympathy, during which I entertain the idea of dialing the phone number Walter Morris has provided. Then I remember the last phone message I got from this brother: "*I hate you, you fucking bitch. Don't pretend like there is anything between us. Fuck you. Don't ever contact me again.*" That was seven or eight years ago, during a brief period I was working on Forgiveness, which was supposed to Free Me from the Past. During that period, I talked to my brother on the phone; or, rather, he talked to me, about his mentally ill life and whoever he believed was persecuting him. When he decided that person was me, the forgiveness experiment ended, and I realized that the best way to free myself was to change my phone number. I was in California, a continent between us, and unless he chose to look me up and come out and find me—possible, though not likely, given the money and engineering it would take to get him out of the pot-wreathed condo in Bethesda our mother had bought him before she died—I could pretty much write him off. I had three other, better brothers.

Now, apparently, he has moved out of the condo. This is Condo Number Two; he accidentally burned down Number One, apparently from falling asleep on the couch with a lit joint, or possibly a cigarette. The fire spread to two other units in the building. There was a lawsuit, and some insurance claims to settle, which our mother took care of. From the real estate situation, you can guess what kind of relationship my mother and oldest brother had, without my needing to provide more examples, like a few totaled and new cars and endless checks made out to him, first in her excellent penmanship and later in the tentative, shivery scrawl of Parkinson's and dementia. Even after she died, the checks, written now by a lawyer, continued for a time. But apparently the well has finally run dry, and my brother is again in need of help.

The phrase in Walter Morris's e-mail that catches my attention is "*his new predicament.*" This suggests they have been in touch for a while, long enough for there to have been several previous predicaments. Whichever one, for example, landed my brother in a small town in North Carolina. I google it and find it's "the fastest-growing city in the state," yet offers "the serenity of small-town living." *Not anymore*, I'm thinking. They're going to have to strike "serenity" and add some antonyms: *agitation, turbulence, violence.* Again, I could provide a few examples, some of which I've used in my fiction. In a short story, I describe a brother who often attacks his sister. Once, he tries to choke her and ends up kicking her repeatedly as she lies on the kitchen floor. He hears voices. He burns down his condo, and the fire spreads to two others. Fiction comes partly from scraps of life stitched together in new patterns; trouble and conflict are its engines, and he is some of the trouble I've experienced in my life.

That my parents took him to a psychiatrist when he was ten years old is telling. They didn't believe in that kind of thing, so it must have been an act of desperation. I don't know what the psychiatrist said. All I knew, as a kid, was that my brother was angry and violent and that, as the only girl, I was the weak one in the herd, given to crying not only from being hit but from the constant stream of toxic adjectives—*ugly*, *stupid*, *spastic*—directed my way. I spent a lot of time hiding in my father's bedroom closet. I got familiar with his shoes, lined up beside the electric silver buffer with its red-and-black brushes. I studied the patterns on his sports jackets and ties, as if they contained some secret to escaping my brother's rage. My mother had a closet, too, but I felt safer among the bigger shoes, inhaling the faint smell of my father's feet and cologne. Also, there was sometimes money in his jacket pockets, which I stole.

"*I am including his phone number.*" I seriously consider calling my brother, but I'm not sure how much I'm motivated by this line of thinking: *Well, he's sixty now, and all that was a long time ago; his friend says it would mean a lot to him. I might be able to alleviate just a little of his suffering.* Or by this one: *I could get some great material out of this. He'll tell me all about his fucked-up life, and I'll use it in some way.*

The second line of thinking feels a little more motivating.

The first feels like simple Christian charity. *Simple*, though, is not one of my go-to adjectives, unless used in a specific context: simple cocktail recipes, say. Nothing in life, especially our relationships with family, is straightforward or easy. There's so much love and pain mixed together, so many grievances held on to or finally let go, bonds that tie us in knots or attenuate to mere threads that can snap, a final sting, then relief and loss and longing and disappointment, all intertwined. *"Please give him a short call."* Just pick up the phone for five minutes, and let the fear and humiliation of your childhood back into your life. As for Christian charity, it conjures—unfairly, I know, but this is what I imagine—groups of badly dressed soldiers for Christ descending on villages in faraway lands to distribute Bibles and gather the starving, big-eyed children for infomercials; it smacks of condescension. Poor people need empowerment, not charity. Had my mother understood that idea in regard to my brother, she might have helped him learn some better survival skills. But he was her firstborn, a pudgy baby with a head of red curls, an obstinate little boy, a cherub in exile. There was something wrong at the center of him, churning like a tornado. There are days I understand that feeling all too well, when I'm spiraling in my own whirlwind, when being inside it is intolerable.

My brother is, or at least was for a while, a God-fearing Christian. The last time I saw him, about ten years ago in the kitchen of our mother's condo—he'd come by to get money for a dental appointment—he was fearing for his immortal soul. "I'm trying to be born again so I can get into heaven," he said. He said of our brother Jon, "He professes Jesus, but he won't get in, because he's divorced." He gave me a pamphlet that told me I was debased, that hell was factual, that the heart was deceitful above all things and beyond cure. "I'm nearly fifty and I'm getting worried," he said. *With good reason*, I thought. Given he'd been eighty-sixed from plenty of tennis tournaments for throwing his racket, sometimes directly at his opponent, it was hard to imagine he'd be welcome in the gated community of the Afterlife. At the time, though, I was glad he'd found the Lord. Let the Church take care of him, and leave our mother alone. She wrote him a check for the dental work. He asked if I wanted to go for drinks later, and I made some excuse. I knew what that would mean: his drinking too much, my wanting to leave before he was ready. Being afraid to insist because there was still the chance he would attack me physically.

Right now, though, he wanted to play the piano for us. He sat at our mother's white baby grand while we assumed postures of interest on the sofa. He was self-taught and played well, though with an overabundance of trills and florid arpeggios. Following the concert he gave a reading of his latest poem, a modern medieval romance. A knight tethered his stallion to a Dr Pepper machine. His lady love's eyes shone like oiled marbles. The knight shook in solitary silence, whispering gently to the bottle top. Next he showed me a *Washington Post* review that he'd penned himself, declaring him "a refreshing voice" and adding that "most of the good poets are dead." He suggested to our mother that he bring a priest over to talk to her about her soul, before it was too late, and she mumbled that she would think about it.

I forward Walter Morris's e-mail to my brother Gary, who, like everyone else in our family, hasn't spoken to him in years.

A minute after I press Send, my phone rings.

"Don't answer the guy," Gary says. "I've heard from a social worker who's trying to unload him on anyone she can."

Apparently, our brother had sold Condo Number Two and run through whatever money he'd made. The social worker had found him a place and a roommate, but he lost the roommate after some sort of violent altercation. "I'm not sure what happened," Gary said. "Someone hit someone with something." This sounded like my oldest brother's MO. He'd once cracked me over the head with a 7Up bottle.

There was more news: He had cancer at some point. He had a kidney removed, and can't walk anymore. (This makes me remember an earlier report, a couple of years before, about him needing a cane to get around. He beat a taxi driver with it.) Now he's in some kind of public housing, living on food stamps. In a few months he'll have to leave and will have no place to go.

When the social worker called Gary, she said, "Everyone I've talked to wants nothing to do with him."

When I used some of my experiences with this brother in my fiction, I thought of it, in a way, as payback. Writing as redemption: the writer gets to shape the story, to remake events. There's a power in that, a sense that you can undo, or at least mitigate, whatever wrongs you've endured. The other party is powerless to stop you. You're telling it, and you can say whatever you want to, need to. But my brother has had his own payback. Call it God's will. Or karma. Or the life he's made or been subject to because of bad brain chemistry and codependent parenting. That black tornado inside him flattening his chances for love, for health, crushing his talent for music and sports.

When his condo burned, so did the tennis trophies he'd accumulated over years of tournament play, gold-plated men melting into their pedestals.

Payback isn't, as it turns out, what I'm after. My writing is about my own life, a part of which includes a brother who loomed large in my childhood, whose swath of destruction cut through our entire family, changing whatever, whoever, we might have been. I don't mourn that imaginary family, the one in which I'm not hiding in the closet or sneaking out to the car with my other brothers to leave behind the one who will ruin the outing. The one in which my parents lose the constant worry and my mother isn't being belittled or attacked. There's no point mourning what never existed. Whatever we're given, we use, or else it destroys us.

My brother terrified me then, and there wasn't a lot I could do about it. I ran away to my best friend's house once, in junior high, but I came back after several days because her parents wouldn't let me stay. When I returned, I tried to confront my mother about what was happening. But confrontations were not anyone's forte, except for my oldest brother and father, and those always involved fists. My mother's advice was this: "Stay out of his way. We can't control him." She was washing the dishes, washing her hands of me. I felt like I was headed for Golgotha.

Then I left home for good at seventeen, and eventually made a creative life for myself.

"I think it would mean a lot to him." Maybe it would. But I'm not going to call my brother. I care what happens to him, and I'm sorry his life has been one long predicament. But I'm free of him now. As a child, I thought I would feel forever the way he made me feel: ugly, worthless, afraid. I didn't know that bad experiences could be outgrown, that you could learn from them the harsh lessons life sometimes imposes, and move on.

Although, maybe I caught a glimpse, one night in high school when he was fighting with our father. It was the usual: "Fuck you, you punk"; "Fuck you too, old man," the two of them lunging at each other, our mother in the middle trying to stop them, the kitchen door left hanging from one hinge. I ran outside into the rain and hid behind the crab apple tree in our front yard, waiting for it to be over. I could still hear them yelling inside, and as usual I worried for my mother, caught between them. It was hot out, despite the downpour. I stood under the canopy of branches, the buds in full pink flower, the branches webbed with sticky white caterpillar cocoons. I thought I might go ahead and sleep there, if the grass beneath the tree stayed dry. My parents would eventually go upstairs to sleep, I knew, but it was harder to predict what my brother would do; he'd pulled me out of bed before, enraged that he couldn't find his tennis shoes, and slammed me against the wall a few times. So I thought it best to stay put for a while.

A few minutes later the front door burst open and my brother ran out. He stopped and stood in the driveway for a minute. Then he doubled over and fell to his knees, moaning, clutching his stomach. It was the onset of the ulcerative colitis that would compromise his health the rest of his life, that would lead to operations, heavy cortisone, a colostomy bag. His muscular, stocky body would grow thin and wasted, his face would get puffy from the cortisone, he would lose everything dear to him. Of course no one knew that then. What I knew that night was that my big bad brother was on his knees in the rain, moaning like a wounded animal, and all I felt for him was pity.

Best Words, Best Order

SOME ENCHANTED EVENING, you see a strange word across a crowded room. It looks different from all the other words; it beckons and glows; it exerts such a powerful magnetism that you are drawn like a murmurous fly to Keats's "*coming musk-rose, full of dewy wine*" in the ode where he feels so happy listening to a nightingale that he thinks about getting drunk, killing himself, and other poetic pursuits.

Those first encounters with language, for a writer, are as powerful as confronting Michelangelo's *Pietà* might be for a budding young artist who previously knew only the lineaments of the molded plastic baby Jesus and kneeling cows in the Christmas crèche dug out yearly from a cardboard box in the basement in Trenton, New Jersey.

For me, discovering the spelling of *bologna* was one such revelatory moment. I was familiar with the thing itself, but not until I saw the word written on a blackboard one Friday in the fourth grade did I appreciate its power. I was instantly hurled into tumultuous confusion about the true nature of reality. How could this ordinary cold cut, pinkish and slippery, trapped between slices of Wonder Bread, slathered with mayonnaise, wrapped in wax paper, and lifted from my Barbie lunchbox each day at school beside the swing set, have such an odd, exotic spelling? Why was there such an enormous distance between the word as it sounded and the way it was actually written? Clearly there were deeper truths than I realized lurking beneath not only language, but existence itself. The routine, mundane occurrences of my nine-year-old world—these were mere appearances, mere shadows on the wall of my bedroom. My human perception was clearly limited. The substance of life might be scarier and wilder than I had imagined. I went around all week with *bologna* in my head and with a new sense of anticipation and dread for the next Friday's spelling and vocabulary list.

But the word that truly rocked my world—a word that made bologna seem like mere Spam—was one that I encountered in a poem the following year. The verse, a simple a-a-b-a quatrain, was written in black Magic Marker on a yellow cement wall in the courtyard of my elementary school. The young bard had written,

> *Her beauty lies*
> *Between her thighs*
> *And that's what makes*
> *My libido rise.*

I had no idea what *libido* meant, but I more or less understood the writer's intent. *Libido*! Maybe it was significant that, like *bologna*, it was a three-syllable word, with that stress, that lift, in the middle. An amphibrach, like *inferno*, or *Dorito*. A Latin word. Foreign, exotic, and in the end—as I discovered, once I got to a dictionary—dirty. It meant sex, desire, excitation. Now the poem itself took hold of me, an intoxicating mix of filth and erudition. It had all the qualities of a great work of literature: paradox, Eros, and the fitting of form to content. The first three lines followed a strict pattern of iambic dimeter. And then the departure, the final line opening into the power of metric substitution, the triple foot of an anapest pouring forth and overflowing its iambic container. The poem met Coleridge's definition of "the best words in the best order." It impressed itself indelibly into memory; once read, it could not be forgotten. I was haunted by the poem, and wondered who the author was. A boy, I was sure—possibly an older man, a sixth-grader. He had stood at that wall; he no doubt stood now somewhere nearby—the tetherball court, or the jungle gym. I burned to find him, a bad boy who understood the subtleties of metrics and knew big words. Who had a libido.

I didn't ever find him. Not in the fifth grade, or in the sixth, when a boy and I crawled into an empty refrigerator box at the back of the classroom—our science project was to construct a spaceship—and made out instead of drawing the control panel. All we had done in there was glue up a picture of some galaxy and stick our tongues in each other's mouths and try not to make any sound that would get us hauled out to drill fractions. He was a good kisser, but when we broke up he wrote a note to a friend that read, "Kim is a pigheaded slob." His language was crude and unrefined, as well as imprecise. The note lacked rhythm, had no surprising metaphor, and its idea was insufficiently developed; it dealt in clichéd generalities (pigheadedness, slobdom) and might have referred to any number of girls named Kim rather than the unique, special eleven-year-old who had allowed his cretinous tongue to slither over her own.

He was the kind of boy I would fall for again and again in the coming years, adorable and unsuitable, ordinary as the dirt in that church in New Mexico that is supposed to heal broken legs and hearts but is really dug up from the hill behind the church and not miraculous at all, which anyone will freely tell you, but people still make pilgrimages and leave their crutches and dog tags hanging there. The guys I fell for rode motorcycles and flew small airplanes and played in bands, and wondered why writers—the writers they knew personally, i.e., me—had to go into things so much. For a while, we would be completely happy together. Then we would grow bored with each other, a circumstance they didn't seem to mind as much as I did. To a man, they married soon after we broke up, except for the one who might be homeless by now.

Then there was the other kind—the kind I did not have to warn not to say "fuck" when we went to lunch at Hamburger Hamlet with my mother. *Fuck* was not a word this man had befriended. But he knew about the roots of jazz or Hindu philosophy or the French Revolution. He admired my poetry; he loved poetry. He understood how Derrida subverted Plato's classical concept of mimesis—there was nothing to be imitated. When he said "hymen," he meant unsettling Heidegger's concept of synthesis, not to mention Lévi-Strauss's Hegelian notion of the third element that mediates between the two members of a binary opposition. I hope you're still with me here. He was brilliant and perfect, except for one little thing: he did not make my libido rise.

All my life, since seeing that perfectly placed word, printed on the wall, I have looked for the one to whom I can say, "Come to me. Call me your little whore and then quote Nietzsche. Tie me up and slap me around and pee on me and then explicate "The Waste Land," granting its status as a seminal work with vast influence on twentieth-century literature without praising it as the impetus for a bunch of postmodern hooey no one can understand. Tell me we're staying in tonight, and whip us up some pan-fried bay scallops and saffron pasta with parsley and garlic, and maybe some white corn cakes with caviar. Let the champagne cork blast loose like a rocket ship and shatter the kitchen light and foam run down your arm while the shards fly. I'll lick the foam while you translate those cuneiform tablets you collected on your last expedition. Dedicate your book and the rest of your carnal life to me, and I'll do the same."

Don't anyone tell me he's not out there, that the perfect admixture of head and heart is a romantic alchemist's fantasy, impossible to achieve. As far as I'm concerned, that's a bunch of bologna. I know he exists. I know.

And listen: if you went to McNab Elementary in Pompano Beach, Florida, and once wrote a poem on a wall, there is someone who wants to meet you.

Don't Worry

"I GOT YOU a couple of presents," Margot said as we stood on the sidewalk outside the blues club in San Francisco, amid a swirl of theatergoers and tourists, next to doorways occupied by the destitute homeless. "But I left them in my hotel room. Do you want to come over? Don't worry, I won't seduce you."

When people tell me they won't seduce me, I believe them. I am credulous. If a man I'd just met were to say to me, "Don't worry, I won't come in you," I would think, *How great that he has thought this through. He's making plans, he's watching out for the roadblocks far ahead on the highway, whereas I am still considering whether to get in the car with him.* It hadn't occurred to me that Margot, my former student, might seduce me, but here she was, letting me know it was a possibility she had considered. Now she was thoughtfully letting me know what would not happen.

Margot had studied with me for about a week at a writers' conference. Here's what I knew about her: She wore a lot of shiny jewelry, had had a piece published in a feminist anthology, and had a novel manuscript that was making the rounds of New York publishers. The day she left home to visit the West Coast, lightning split a tree in her yard. She used the word *cleaved*. Also, she wanted to create an action doll named Booberella. "Maybe one of those bobble-headed dolls," she'd said in the club earlier.

"Or maybe the breasts could be on springs instead," I said.

"Bobble-boobs," she said. "Good idea."

"Definitely marketable," I said.

I was out with Margot on a Saturday night because I didn't have a date. Single men seemed to have grown scarce since my last breakup. I looked around the club: couples everywhere. We drank Lemon Drops and ripped through a pile of yam fries, and then Margot introduced me to a liqueur called Apfelkorn, which she said could be used to make drinks with interesting names like Appletini, Apple Fucker, and Fuck in the Graveyard. I wondered how one fucked an apple. All I knew was how to make a pipe out of an apple in order to smoke pot. I'd learned that right before going to the Bread Loaf Writers' Conference one year and taught it to a number of people there. Fucking in a graveyard was easier to imagine, though I'd never done it. Once, years ago, I had swing-danced on my father's grave with a man I liked. Maybe, I thought, I should move to New York, where that man is living, and see if he is single now. The last time I'd seen him he'd been with his new wife, but I could tell it wasn't going to last long.

I got a little drunk on the Appletinis. The harmonica player in the band was standing on a table, blowing like mad and delighting the crowd, and I wanted to curl up into a small dark space, maybe under that table, and sleep for a year or two. I thought about the "sleep cure" in *Valley of the Dolls*, a book I read as a preteen that moved me deeply and educated me in the ways of pathologically damaged women. Maybe there was a doctor who could help me. And if I couldn't get a sleep cure, maybe I could be admitted to the hospital with a broken wrist or something, develop a mysterious infection, and be put into an induced coma. One day, passing my bed, a handsome new doctor would fall in love with my tube-covered face, lean over, and put his tongue in my mouth, and my new life would begin.

Meanwhile, here was Margot, staggering on the sidewalk from drunkenness, or pain; she had turned her ankle on a broken piece of sidewalk.

"Looks like we're going to need a cab," I said, and instantly one magically rolled out of a parking garage and stopped for us.

Margot's hotel room was small, most of it filled by the bed, so I sat on the bed. She brought out a tube of glitter gel and a puzzle cube with several images of Frida Kahlo on it. Frida stabbed and bleeding, Frida with parrots and monkeys and dogs, the black wings of her eyebrows meeting. Frida and Diego Rivera had a typical marriage for two sensitive artists: passion, pain, professional jealousy, and the indiscriminate bedding of other sensitive artists and intellectuals.

"Thank you," I said. "These are great presents. And, wow, you have a mini bar."

Margot was already opening the chardonnay. She brought

me a glass and sat on the bed next to me. She trailed her fingers along my arm. "Is this okay?" she said.

I wasn't feeling anything like erotic attraction, since I was generally pretty sure I was heterosexual, but maybe these things took time; maybe I could make this work. I took a sip of my wine. We were reclining on the bed by now, and I was looking into her cleavage, lightly dusted with glitter, where a pendant of some kind nestled. Possibly it had supernatural powers; I was starting to feel sleepy. Soon I might fall into a light trance and remember my past life as Cleopatra.

"What time is it?" I said. "I don't want to miss my BART train." BART stopped running about midnight. I felt like I was in some fractured version of "Cinderella." "Lesbian Cinderella"? "Cinderlesbian"? Cinderella attends the blues ball with Princess Booberella, who trips in her glass slippers and then whisks Cinderella to her hotel room in a coach driven by a Serbian, who denounces the machinations of wicked King Bush and his rat Cabinet as they speed through the neon streets of the kingdom.

"We have this connection," Princess Booberella said. Or maybe she said, "I feel this connection," or possibly, "Feeling is connection." This is the part that gets a little fuzzy in my memory. I remember her taking off my cowboy boots and then touching me a little more, each time with an "Is this okay?" and my mumbled "*Um, ah.*" I think my breasts were the goal, the hills to be taken. On the plains, the guerrillas crept closer, alert for mines, for snipers. I thought about junior high, making out with boys who slowly, with the wild stealth of adolescence, worked their way from my shoulder down toward the top of my blouse. I still wasn't feeling anything except a slight tickling sensation that made me want to scratch where she had touched me. But I thought scratching would be impolite, so I tried to develop a meditative frame of mind where nothing bothered me, like the woman who wrote about being perfectly serene while getting bitten by mosquitoes in India.

"Okay," Margot said, stopping before she had breached my bra. Maybe she was going to call in an air strike.

"Now you do something to me," she said, and leaned back on the bed.

I felt way too self-conscious to do anything to Margot. Suddenly I wished I were at home, alone, having my usual weekend-long marathon of depression and envy. Friday and Saturday nights, I thought of all the couples going out to dinner and to clubs; Sunday mornings, I thought of them staying late in bed together, frolicking in the sheets, then going for champagne brunch, followed by a hike or bike ride or a stroll through a local farmers' market, smelling damp bouquets of flowers, squeezing peaches, choosing fresh breads and pastries. I was my own Self-Pity Party in a Box. Maybe I could market it: a solitaire deck featuring photos of happy couples, a bottle of cheap whiskey, a Lucinda Williams CD with those songs about losing her joy and the guy who never made her come. For a little extra I could personalize it with your wedding video and your ex's voice mail greeting.

I thought about *cleave*, a word that means to cling to, but also to separate. It's a perfect word for ambivalence. I was alone and hated it, but I hadn't taken any concrete steps toward finding someone. I was a Kim Puzzle Cube. Not one of me was smiling. It occurred to me that I could choose to go on being in pieces over my last relationship, or I could choose to go out and look for another one. I could even sleep with a woman, if I really wanted to. Freedom was mine.

I sat up and put on my boots. "I need to go," I said. I got off the bed, feeling a little dizzy. I'd barely touched the chardonnay, so it must have been the Appletinis. "Thank you for the presents. I'm getting a cab back to BART."

"Are you sure?" Margot said.

I looked at her, a lovely young woman lying back on a hotel bed. But she wasn't what I wanted. I left her there, glittery and ready, a beautiful vision that remains in my head.

Bukowski in a Sundress

THE NATIONAL BOOK Critics Circle Award committee was meeting to discuss noteworthy books and had winnowed them down to a longlist of ten. One of my poetry collections was on the list. According to the minutes of the meeting, which I found online, one judge characterized me as *"Charles Bukowski in a sundress."* Given the level of regard Bukowski enjoys in prestigious literary circles, it's hard to believe this was meant as a compliment. In any case, in the next round of voting, my book was winnowed right out.

Frankly, I'd have preferred a different, though equally nuanced, characterization of my work—say, "Gerard Manley Hopkins in a bomber jacket," or "Walt Whitman in a sparkly tutu," or possibly "Emily Dickinson with a strap-on." But this is what happens when you put your work out into the world—if you're lucky. If you're not lucky, no one says anything at all, because no one knows that your slim little volume of poetry or your novel ten years in the making even exists.

I used to google myself and read what people said about me on their blogs. This is a bad idea if you want to maintain the illusion that people are seriously reading your poems and understanding more than 17 percent of what you are trying to be up to. Undergraduate student papers attempting to assay your oeuvre are especially scary. At least the students have the excuse of youth and ignorance. Who can be expected to get poetry at that tender age? Only those who are already little existentialists, aware of the innate meaninglessness of life, staring into the void in fascination, lonely and stoned out of their heads—that is, future poets.

Once you are a published writer, open season has been declared on you, all year long, for the rest of your life. Of course, writers aren't celebrities; we're not the kind of big game that adventurers go on safari to shoot, or even the deer that ordinary hunters are so fond of picking off. Maybe we're more like the scimitar-horned oryx—exotic, endangered, but still occasionally caught in the crosshairs of pumped-up sportsmen high on whiskey and the rush of killing an innocent wild animal.

If you are at all successful, there are people who will automatically envy, hate, and belittle you. Usually these people will be other writers who are less successful. The other day, I saw an enormous poster on a bus stop advertising a bestselling author's novel. I happen to know that this author is a very nice person, but at that moment the shriveled, jealous creature in me wanted her to die, immediately and violently.

If you are a female poet, a lot of male wannabe poets will pen lines of crappy verse making it sound as though they spent a blissful night of love with you, and there is nothing you can do about it. They are like those boys in high school who told everyone you were a slut and then, when they caught you on the hall stairs alone after class, tried to stick their hands down your pants. They are retromingent Visigoths, which means self-pissing barbarians. I stole the phrase from a long-ago *New Yorker* article having something to do with sports, and I've found it useful to have in the lexicon.

Most male critics, the ones who will write about your work as if it were the source of the *Vagina dentata* myth, are also retromingent Visigoths. Many of them may also be victims of a serious brain disorder. What happens is this: the text, which for a normal person is processed through thoughtful reading, instead enters a series of wormholes deep in the temporal lobes. These wormholes destroy the amygdalae, which are essential for the processing of memory and emotion. It's as though your writing becomes trapped in a fun house of warped, distorting mirrors, where it stumbles around, barely recognizable, bumping into ventricles. The ventricles, which ordinarily carry spinal fluid, in this case are filled with bile. Here is one thing you can do, if your work is reviewed by one of these critics: tape a photocopied picture of his face above a paper dress, cut up the doll with manicure scissors, and set it on fire, preferably in a public forum such as a writers' conference. I personally found this cathartic.

I keep meaning to really read Bukowski one of these days. I've seen a poem here and there, and my main reaction was *meh.* Though I read a good one once in *Poetry* magazine. I know he wrote about sex and drinking and fighting and whores, and that he said that most poetry was overly precious trash. He said a number of other things I agree with, like this: "An intellectual says a simple thing in a hard way. An artist says a hard thing in a simple way." And this: "We're all going to die, all of us, what a circus! That alone should make us love each other but it doesn't. We are terrorized and flattened by trivialities, we are eaten up by nothing." Those statements made me like him, in that way you can like someone you'll never have to meet. More than forty of his sixty-odd books are still in print. That's an enviable statistic, but there's no point wishing him dead, since he already is.

Recently I thought it might be a good idea to get to know Bukowski better. There wasn't a bookstore within miles, and I wanted to get started right away, so I clicked over to Netflix to watch a movie based on some of his stories. I opened a beer, to better identify with my research subject, and settled down to watch *Tales of Ordinary Madness* starring Ben Gazzara.

There are a couple of standout lines in the film that I'm pretty sure Bukowski actually wrote. "Touch my soul with your cock" is one that made me spit Heineken all over myself. But even better was the description of a woman whom the main character—one of the versions of Bukowski who stumble through his stories—follows home: "She had an ass like a wild animal." I wish he'd been a little more specific there, though, since the asses of animals can differ significantly; was her ass more like that of a naked mole rat, or a feral dog, or possibly a vagrant shrew? I'm not sure which wild animal a man would be more likely to follow off a bus, but maybe I'm being unfairly literal here.

The seeker of the soul-touching cock is a gorgeously vapid girl with no discernible personality, so when she kills herself, late in the film, it's tough to feel the loss. It's kind of like a potted plant has died. And the aforementioned ass belongs to a pretty unlikely character. It's not that women don't flirt with strangers they let follow them home, and then enact all manner of sex games, including bondage, fake rape, and lying spread-legged on the floor pretending to be dead in the hope of being fucked senseless, followed by actual fucking and then calling the cops to press charges while the hapless lover enjoys a cigar and a bubble bath, thinking she's out there rustling up a romantic dinner. Of course women occasionally do those things, and probably Bukowski encountered a stellar representative of this branch of female desire. But nothing about her rings true, either because the actress overdoes it, or—my suspicion—there's not much to base her character on, only actions and reactions, as though some freak sexual chemical experiment has produced her. That is, she seems a poorly written creature. And, bludgeon me over the head after fake-raping me, but I have a problem with men who can't write female characters. Don't tell me I should actually read Bukowski instead of watching a movie and then spouting some simplistic, politically correct, ovary-inflected criticism; like I said, published writers are fair game.

I cracked another beer and settled back to watch a documentary about Bukowski. There was some footage of him giving readings, getting wasted on beers from an onstage re-frigerator or guzzling wine from a bottle on a table. There were big audiences, laughing and hooting at the spectacle of an addict showcasing his intimate relationship with his drug of choice. It was a little like bear baiting. Then again, he seemed like someone who practiced self-acceptance rather than the guilt and self-loathing that drive so many lesser alcoholics into AA. He never quit. He went on drinking and wrote book after book.

So even though I suspect that critic was being a dick about my work, I've decided I'm going to be proud of my new nickname. If I am truly honest with myself, I have to admit that I have always wanted someone to touch my soul with his cock. Since childhood, I have wondered where my soul was, and I'm glad to discover it's up there somewhere in my lady parts.

And who knows. Maybe one day, when Bukowski's up for a posthumous literary award, some critic will say, "Oh, him? Kim Addonizio in pee-stained pants," and then I hope whoever said it pukes on his shoes.

Cocktail Time

EVERYONE THINKS THAT being a writer disposes one toward heavy drinking. Like all ideas about writers, this statement contains some truth, adulterated with gossip and the romantic fantasies of young aspiring writers. The truth is that we spend an inordinate amount of time at our work, which means we spend our time alone, in a room of our own if we're lucky, and in the worlds in our heads. Depending on your feelings about solitude, and your own inner life, you may understand why some of us enjoy the company of spirits.

If you think it's amazing that humans have up to thirty feet of intestines coiled in our bodies, think about the galaxies and planets, the supernovas and black holes that exist in writers' heads. If we want an occasional cocktail to help us cope with the vastness of space, don't give us a hard time.

Go get a wheatgrass enema and drink your herbal tea. Be healthy and happy, and do not dwell on the past, the future, imaginary people in parallel universes, or what might have been. See how much work you get done.

My friend Elizabeth invented a drink she called the E-tini. Once, when I was asked to contribute a recipe to a food and drink anthology, I included her drink and invented my own, the K-tini. Here they both are:

Two Quick-and-Dirty Drink Recipes to Get You Quickly Dirty

THE E-TINI

Into a glass, flask, juice jar, paper cup, hollowed coconut shell, or other suitable container such as cupped hands (having a partner for this last will prove useful), pour:

⅓ Absolut vanilla vodka, fresh from the freezer
⅓ cold orange juice
⅓ cold pineapple juice
Top with a floater of the Absolut. Do not stir.
Drink immediately.

The E-tini tastes like a Dreamsicle. It's simple, refreshing, and full of sugar, but you can feel good that you are drinking two kinds of juice. If you wish to bypass feeling good and go straight to feeling fucked up, try the K-tini.

THE K-TINI

1. Open freezer and remove any hard alcoholic beverage.
2. Unscrew cap.
3. Open mouth and apply to bottle.
4. Swallow as many times as possible before stopping to inhale.

Wine from the refrigerator or cupboard may be substituted for 1; in that case, however, the characteristic and oft-mentioned "kick" of the K-tini can't be experienced. Wine is for wannabes. The K-tini is the drink for those in the know, those who are sick with thirst, whose demons are swarming. Your demons snicker at wine, at lite beer, at bitters and soda. Give them what they clamor for: give them K-tinis. Feel so fucked up you fall to the floor, hitting your head on your marble counter. When you wake up, put on your sexiest online Victoria's Secret purchase and dance wildly before your full-length mirror, then collapse sobbing into a pile of soiled underwear, weeping because there is no one to see how hot you look. Decide to go to the bar; have another K-tini before you leave, then get behind the wheel. Don't stop for the car you sideswipe or the kitten you mow down. Drive! Drive! Your true love is waiting for you. You'll be together forever, as soon as you hit that tree.

Penis by Penis

"Oh, Mom, get online," my daughter said. "That's how everybody meets these days."

"Really?"

"Yeah, pretty much." Aya met her own boyfriend at a New York restaurant where she was waitressing between acting jobs.

"Really," I said again. And here I thought you just went into a bar, had several drinks, and emerged a few hours later with a new boyfriend. But my previous MO had stopped working at some point. I spent my days alone, writing, answering e-mail, reading student poems. I went to the gym and clamped on my headphones and spoke to no one; and to yoga class, where the teacher said, "Lift head, lift heart," dropping articles and possessive pronouns. There was no one appealing lifting head and heart on the next yoga mat. And no sexy, sensitive man was jogging on the treadmill or bench-pressing his chest into a rock-hard slab where I could lay my head.

I tried going out alone at night to restaurants where I could sit at the bar with a book and eat dinner and maybe strike up an acquaintance with the love of my life. Around me swirled the meaningless, mindless conversations of the happily connected, couples and groups of friends merrily raising neon cocktails while I took out my reading glasses and hunched over Cormac McCarthy's *The Road*, a novel about trying to survive in a bleak, ash-covered world where most of the humans are dead, and the ones who are left may attack and eat you. Also, I noticed, the clientele had gotten a lot younger than in the days I used to frequent bars regularly and meet men willing to follow me home and begin a serious relationship.

So I finally cast my net into the waters of online dating. But it turned out I was casting it in some distant part of the ocean, where few men my age were to be found. They were all nibbling at the profiles of younger women. If they were my age, fifty-three, they were looking for someone thirty-three to forty-five. In my part of the ocean, there were a lot of women sitting around on their boats with nothing to do but chain-smoke cigarettes or drink wine or teach their cat a few simple tricks.

Still, it turned out there were a handful of men who wanted to date me. I am very photogenic. This is not always a good thing. Once, in Berkeley Rep before a theater performance, I saw that the guy behind the counter in the gift store was reading one of my books, so I sidled over. He looked up at me blankly; when I told him I was the author, he looked from the author photo to me like someone at the morgue, trying to match the living person he remembered to the thing he was confronted with: a bloated corpse pulled from a refrigerated drawer.

I narrowed the several responses I'd received down to two. Maybe I had too many criteria. Maybe I truly wasn't ready. It had been over two years since a long-term relationship had ended—two lonely, penis-deprived years. I missed the penis. But I couldn't seem to bite the bullet, so to speak, and blithely go out and meet a bunch of strangers. Anne Lamott suggested that writers proceed "bird by bird," describing a research paper on birds her little brother was overwhelmed by the prospect of starting. *Okay*, I thought. *I'll just take it penis by penis.*

The first one, Evan, was thirty-nine. Fourteen years younger, and he was interested in me! This meant (a) he thought I'd be easy to bag, or (b) he didn't care about my age, or (c) both. He sent his phone number and invited me to call.

"Uh, hi," I said one night when I'd had a little wine for courage. I felt like a telemarketer, trying not to get hung up on before I could pitch theater tickets or alumni contributions.

"Who's this?" he said.

"Kim. From. . . . the Yahoo! Personals."

"Oh," he said.

I knew I should have prepared a script, so I would know what to say and could anticipate his responses. It would go something like this:

ME: Hey, Evan! It's Kim from the Personals! Like, how's it going? Wow, I'm at this party right now and a girl just puked on herself—I am so outta here. I'm going clubbing. What are you up to?

EVAN: Ah, just chillin', you know.

ME: Cool! Let's hook up! I'm right in the city. Man, these Appletinis have me blasted out of my mind. I'm, like, ready to fuck in a graveyard or something. Also, I just took some X, and I've got an extra hit in my bra. Unless I swallow it in the meantime.

EVAN: Cool. I'll be there in half an hour.

ME: I'll text you the address. I'll be the one in the really short dress, laughing my ass off at the bar. Woo-*hoo*!

"So . . . ," I said, in real life. "Just thought I'd call and say hi."

"I'm in Florida," Evan said.

"Oh, really!" I wondered if I could hang up now and end the evening with just a small spoonful of humiliation, rather than the heaping portion I sensed was coming. "How come you're in Florida?"

"Visiting family," he said.

Evan seemed to be a man of few words. Why had he asked me to call him, if he wasn't going to talk to me? And what did I have to say to him? Apparently, nothing. "Oh," I said. "When will you be back?"

"I'm not sure."

Now I felt more like a suspicious wife, the kind who calls the bar demanding to know if her husband is there. The bartender says no, and exchanges a smirking look with the husband.

"Oh. Well, I just called to say hi . . ." I was sitting at one end of my couch. I looked at my shelves of books. Novels, short story collections, poetry anthologies, words and more words. If only he would ask me something about writing, like *"Do you keep a schedule?"* or *"Who are your influences?"* He could ask me what, exactly, Keats said about Negative Capability, and I would answer immediately, "Capable of being in uncertainties, mysteries, doubts, without any irritable reaching after fact and reason." Maybe we could discuss the identity of the Dark Lady in Shakespeare's sonnets, or John Berryman's use of persona in *The Dream Songs*.

Silence on the other end. Maybe I should initiate phone sex. We could talk dirty and have simultaneous orgasms, and then arrange to meet for a quick coffee at Starbucks to see if we actually wanted to date.

"Thanks for calling," he said.

"You asked me to give you a call," I said, "so . . ."

"Yeah," he said.

"Okay, well, guess we'll meet one of these days."

"Bye," Evan said. "Bye" meant *Never.* It meant, *As far as you are concerned, I have disappeared like the dinosaurs,* and *If you ever dial this number again, a hypersonic charge will come through the phone line to electrocute you.*

That left Tom: mid-fifties, liked literature, had a photo of himself with his Lotus race car. Over e-mail, we discussed race cars and gardening, two subjects I wasn't particularly conversant with. I learned that a Lotus had once won the Le Mans, whatever that was. I told him I was growing brussels sprouts on my deck. The brussels sprouts were an experiment to see if a living vegetable could get within fifty feet of me and survive. So far I had been responsible for the deaths of several tomato vines and some broccolini. Tom seemed like an interesting guy. There were a lot of interesting guys online whom I might want to date if I were able to get past their looks, which I was not. I was a shallow, disgusting excuse for a person; I craved beautiful men and I killed vegetables. Tom, at least from his online photo, looked attractive.

Finally he wrote, *"Wanna spoil this and get together?"*

We met at one of the restaurants where I'd tried sitting at the bar alone. Now I was one of the happy couples. Maybe everyone in the restaurant was actually in the same situation as I was, meeting the person across the table for the first time. I looked around; it was hard to tell. It was possible that all these people had ended an important long-term relationship and had been floundering for some time, and were connected for only this one moment. At the end of the evening they would go home alone, hating online dating even more than their loneliness.

When we'd been talking five minutes, my date suddenly leaned over and sniffed me.

"You smell good," he said.

Only he didn't simply lean close; he wedged his nose

into my armpit, like a dog getting a thorough whiff of another dog or checking out an appealing mound of trash. I pulled back and reached for my neon cocktail.

"Thank you," I said. This is what I usually say when I am at a loss. I am like someone in a foreign country who knows a phrase or two of the local language and keeps repeating it, hoping to get by. *Thank you for the traffic ticket. Thank you for the bad highlights that ruined my hair. Thank you for sniffing me, instead of stabbing me.*

"You dick," the woman on a barstool to my right said, but she wasn't saying it to my date; she had her own.

"So you write poetry," Tom said. "I've met a lot of poets. I met some Nobel laureates. I've known some movie stars, too."

I wondered if he had sniffed these people as well, or if he reserved that for online dates.

"I've traveled the world," Tom said. "I almost went up on the Space Shuttle once. I invented a cure for cancer, but the government killed my research grant."

As he steered the conversation into the speculative waters of mind control and alien abductions, it occurred to me that my date might be mentally ill. Also, he pretended not to know who I was, but it turned out that he did. Finally he said that he knew my work, a little. When he started to analyze my character on the basis of particular poems, quoting my lines to me, I started feeling a little faint.

"I think I need to go home now," I said. "Wow, these drinks went to my head."

"I'll walk you to the parking lot."

"Thank you," I said. *Thank you, you stalker.* I'd had stalkers before. They read my poems and felt they knew me intimately. They sent long, rambling e-mails, or letters with photographs of themselves with their former lovers' heads scissored out and mine inserted. They sent epic poems about our imagined nights of sexual bliss. I once wrote a poem about a red dress; a lot of the poems people sent were about how they would take the dress off me and what we would do together afterward. One man offered to let me stay at his house in Idaho and sent me a check for fifty dollars along with a brochure about his own life's work: tape recordings of murderers' confessions. A young woman started a voluminous one-sided correspondence with me and came to a couple of readings, and when I gave her a casual hello, she got upset because I addressed her by the wrong name. YOU ARE DEAD TO ME was the subject line of her next e-mail.

At my car, Tom leaned in to kiss me, and I turned my cheek. When I turned my head back, he managed to land a kiss on my lips before I could move them out of striking range.

The next day, he called my cell phone. I looked at the number as the phone rang. I waited for it to go to voice mail. Then I e-mailed him that I didn't think it was going to work out, and I took my profile offline, despite having paid over eighty dollars for six months.

But penises are like buses, right? There's bound to be another one chugging up the road soon. Then again, maybe they are, after all, like birds. Maybe I should put a feeder out in the yard, hoping to attract one before they all fly off into the trees, into other women's arms. There are plenty of penises in the world, numerous as the small birds dotting the light poles and telephone wires. And some nights, I think I can hear the one meant for me, singing its heart out into the darkness, not knowing I'm listening, but hoping I am.

DOA

MY NEW NOVEL was being dictated by God. If I left my desk even to pee I'd lose whole pages, the words were streaming in so fast. Forget stopping for lunch. Who needed food? I wasn't a human anymore, a gross, fleshly creature that had to eat or die. I was a vehicle for divine prophecy, electrical impulses pulsing through me and into my Word document. I knew my main character, knew her story, could intuit the whole structure of the book, a glowing constellation. There were Lyra, Andromeda, Perseus, Pegasus, Vulpecula, and Ursa Major, and there, in the night sky above my desk, blazed Kim's Amazing New Novel.

What a load of shit I just told you.

Here's what was really happening: I was paralyzed with despair. I had rewritten my opening a dozen times. My main character was drunk on the eve of her fortieth birthday, standing on a kitchen chair, her head in the freezer. No, she was wasted in the middle of the afternoon, lying in bed in her underwear, watching Oprah comfort a hurricane survivor. No, wait! It was the morning of her birthday. She sat in the kitchen with a pounding hangover, watching her unfaithful husband juice carrots. Or else she was at the party where she fell down drunk after taking her future husband into the bathroom, blowing out the candle on the back of the toilet, and kissing him. Wait. Wait. She was at a fancy organic restaurant with her husband and two other people, slamming the wine, forgetting the niceties of sniffing or swirling, since one of the other people was the young, perky little bitch of an actress her unfaithful husband was sleeping with. Or about to be sleeping with. But maybe that was totally wrong. And the unfaithful husband—wait, should he be the faithful husband, after all? I'd already saddled my character with a bipolar father and a habit of self-medicating her depression. Maybe it was a bad idea to make the husband such a dick. Maybe the four of them should just have a healthful overpriced meal, get drunk, and go home. Happy birthday, main character. Now fuck off.

The drinking part: at least I was sure about that. I wanted to start drinking right then, first thing in the morning, I felt so hopeless about my novel. My third novel. Shouldn't I know how to do this by now? Didn't I have confidence in my abilities, after those novels were published by a big corporate house that had paid me pretty decent money? I was a novelist. That meant I could write novels. *Novel, novel, novel*—it occurred to me that the word also meant "new." As in, *You are so new, you clueless idiot.*

Writing a novel is like having a baby. I know, because I've had both, and the experiences were hellish. By comparison, the tortures of the damned—plunged into excrement, boiled in blood, beheaded, set upon by harpies—are like love nips from your yippy little dog.

I had natural childbirth, which, in hindsight, was a strange decision for someone who had willingly ingested a lot of drugs in her young life to numb the pain and social anxiety of pre-adolescence, adolescence, and then adulthood. There was pot, mescaline, acid, quaaludes, Seconals, coke, heroin, speed, and probably a few more that don't spring as readily to mind. But when it came to childbirth, I didn't take a thing. I screamed, panting like a dog per birth class instructions, squatting on the floor of the Natural Childbirth Center in the hospital after the doctor made me get off the toilet because he was afraid the baby might just whoosh out into the bowl. Instead, the baby whooshed into the waiting hands of the doctor, squatting right down there with me, and my ordeal ended.

And was immediately forgotten, after I'd walked shakily to the bed and lain down, and the nurse delivered my wrinkled, blood-covered, sublimely perfect and unconscionably beautiful baby girl into my arms.

In starting my third novel, I had forgotten all the sweat and difficulty that had gone into the first two. I'd forgotten how much true work it takes—at least for me—to get anything right. Not that I hadn't worked on this novel. In fact, I'd done quite a bit of work already. I'd written a first draft in about ten weeks, propelled by anxiety. I can't stand being inside a long piece of writing; I'm always afraid I won't be able to finish it. So I go as fast as I can toward the finish. Even if the draft sucks, which it always does, I have to have a beginning, middle, and end before I can work on anything. With shorter pieces, I can hold the whole thing in my head. I can get my sucky draft down quickly, and then go back and give it an Extreme Makeover.

For the next two years I wrote more drafts, fixing things—a little rhinoplasty, some cheek implants, liposuction for the fatty modifiers. Finally I gave it to my agent, made some more changes based on his suggestions, and he submitted it to the publisher who had brought out my first two novels.

Done deal, right? I'd worked plenty; I'd broken a sweat, not remembering that with the other books, I had soaked through my clothes, the sheets, the blankets. Don't tell me that was early menopause. With those books, I had obsessed over my characters, scribbled charts of intersecting lines trying to figure out the arc of each one, put one away for three years because I couldn't face the challenges. I had forgotten that I always think something is ready before it truly is. I had forgotten the pain of childbirth, the best description of which I once heard from another young mother: "It's like trying to pass a hot toaster oven through your bowels." I blithely sent my manuscript off to my agent and waited for my editor to send some breathless superlatives my way.

"*I'm afraid I can't find the beating heart of this book*," my editor—now known as my former editor—e-mailed my agent.

She had pronounced my novel DOA. It was lifeless on a gurney, drained of fluids; it wasn't worth much, except maybe to new medical students who would learn how to open it up and try not to gag or retch as they studied what was inside. It was going to be buried in a plain box in an unmarked grave with all the other failed novels.

At least it would have a lot of company. The cemetery is large, the mounds of dirt many. There are thousands of hopeful books that have been pronounced dead by New York editors. All over the cemetery, aspiring novelists are standing or kneeling, remembering their would-be books, laying bouquets of lilies or a single rose. Probably a lot of those novels are clawing the insides of their coffins, beating their fists against the wood, crying out, *But I'm alive! I want to live!*

The thing is, I'd already gotten a partial advance. A book advance is like manna from heaven. You gather it up, praise the baffling and transcendent ways of the gods of New York publishing, and spend it. You pay off your Visa bill and your back taxes and get some needed dental work. Soon I was my usual broke self again. Unless I could radically rewrite my novel into something my agent could sell, I would have to find that manna to pay back my publisher. Or else yank my new gold crowns out of my mouth and melt them down.

According to my former editor, the main character in my novel was too passive. Too much happened *to* her. A passive character is death to a story. The first question to ask is, *What does your character want? What is keeping her from getting it?* Also, it may be generally a good idea if your character is likable, which in a New York editor's mind, as far as I can tell, usually means that he or she is spunky, or brave, possibly funny, and hopefully in possession of in-depth knowledge of the world of high fashion or Alsatian cooking or Freemasonry or time travel. Having an unusual family—say, one of beekeeping undertakers—might also be a plus. Forget ordinary life. Have your character speak from beyond the grave, another planet, or an alternative dimension full of magnetically luscious supernatural creatures. Some bloodsucking sex scenes would be great. Make the retarded boy in your story a demon, put him in an outhouse with a blind tiger, and give him the mission of enslaving the earth. Your book will sell at auction for a high six figures.

This was my rationalization for not acknowledging her critique of my character: *What does she know? I am an unrecognized genius.*

Then I thought about how pointless it was to write another book. There were thousands of books already, all of them desperately trying to get into the hands of readers. They were like baby sea turtles, hatched from eggs buried in the sand, digging their way up to the surface of the beach and scrambling toward the open sea while the masses of hungry shorebirds picked them off one by one and swallowed them whole. My first novel, *Little Beauties*, did pretty well. It was even optioned for a film. The second novel's sales were disappointing. For this, of course, I blame my publisher.

Was I really up, though, for trying again to write this novel?

I have three little words for you: *Twenty thousand dollars.*

So I went back and started rewriting the opening. Some days, I avoided looking at the stack of pages on my desk, hoping it would magically transform itself into something that resembled a finished manuscript. Elves would come in the night and do the work I wasn't capable of. They would figure out the Arc, fix the problems with the plot, and shoot up my character with crystal meth, if need be, making her get off her ass and become the heroine, instead of the victim, of her life.

One day, I sat down and reread a couple of paragraphs. I hated them. They weren't even bad. They were just insipid— too dull for, well, words, as though they had been dictated by the doddering vice president of a ball bearings manufacturing company. I had worked for this man once, my left foot on the pedal of something called a Dictaphone, typing the letters he sent about the importance of ball bearings. I was the slave of this machine, chained to a desk, wearing clothes I'd borrowed from my roommate to create a Front Desk Appearance, though no one ever entered the office except the guys headed to the warehouse in back.

> Dear Blah,
> Blah blah ball bearings blah blah blah.
> > Sincerely,
> > Vice President Blah

This was my novel.

But years ago I made a commitment to writing. Sickness and health. Richer and cracking open champagne for the first twenty-five copies of my first-ever bona fide novel; poorer and skipping dental appointments. So I started rewriting again.

And again. It was like passing a hot toaster oven through my bowels, but I did it, finally—I finished the book, and saw it published.

What another load of shit.

I never finished the book. It took a few years to pay back the advance. I haven't looked at that novel in ages. I don't know if I'll ever return to it and try to raise the dead, to set my zombie novel walking toward a few readers to eat their brains in a way they'll enjoy. Maybe I'll steal some scenes and use them elsewhere. Maybe not. The one thing that is true: I'm still a writer. And sometimes writers fail. No matter how hard we work, there are projects that don't pan out—poems, stories, and even entire books. When the full moon rises over the cemetery, those projects haunt us and torment our sleep.

Still, here's how I've found writing sometimes works: if you are madly avoiding one genre, your imagination may suddenly kick in elsewhere. I couldn't face my novel, so I fled to short stories for solace. I found them beautiful, memorable, moving, harrowing, uplifting—and blessedly short. I'd published a collection years before, written a few more stories, and stopped for several years. Now I wondered how I could have abandoned this form, so full of the human drama, able to create entire lives in just a few pages. How could I have forgotten Denis Johnson's *Jesus' Son* or Jayne Anne Phillips's *Black Tickets* or the seductions of Mary Gaitskill and Lydia Davis, Paul Bowles and Edward P. Jones? What about Wharton and Chekhov? What about Aimee Bender, David Means, George Saunders, Tobias Wolff, and hundreds of other astounding, ass-kicking practitioners—they were everywhere, strewing flowers across the bitter landscape of my failure.

So I got to work and revised some earlier stories. I threw out others that were simply not good enough. Everywhere I looked, I saw possibilities. I listened to bar patrons and cab drivers and friends and people I met at parties, and to my own memories and obsessions and fantasies, and characters came to me, sometimes shyly, sometimes eagerly, all of them saying, *"Tell my story. It won't take long. Sometimes you spend a brief period of time with someone, and that person changes your life forever."*

And ten years after I had abandoned stories, I had a viable collection.

I sold my book, *The Palace of Illusions*, to an editor who said he loved it. Okay, there are some likable characters. Some of them are funny and know about things like carnival life or professional ice skating or Byzantine architecture. There is also one little bloodsucking sex scene. But I'd like to think that the book's exploration of the fun house mirrors we encounter as we struggle to make sense of our lives is what spoke to the editor, someone who cared as much as I had come to care, again, about the power and elegance of the short story.

Imagine a woman, alone and busy writing in a borrowed beach house on the Pacific, getting the call that tells her she has just sold a story collection. She hangs up, a big smile plastered on her face. She's about to have a margarita and watch a few deer browsing in the tall grass on the spit of land that separates her from the ocean. The sun is easing under the horizon, a breeze is kicking up, and—I shit you not—our heroine is happy, feeling lucky in her chosen work.

How to Fall for a Younger Man

HE'S LOUNGING ON your couch, a bottle of beer held between his thighs. You've gotten together to play some music
after meeting in a blues band workshop. You'd been playing
harmonica alone for years, and were ready, if not for the big
time, at least to try the next step. During ten weeks of practice and a performance, you thought of him as *that kind-
of-cute young guy*. You weren't remotely interested then; you
were too busy freaking out about your playing. When he came
over with his guitar tonight, mostly what you thought about
was how tentative he seemed, how lacking in self-assurance.
This was pretty much how you felt, too, as you struggled together to find some musical common ground. In the band, he
had played lead guitar, laying down searing licks on his Tele-
caster, but now you are trying to be an acoustic duo, and it's a
whole different story.

You walk toward him, carrying your beer. You sit at the opposite end of the couch, and all of a sudden you notice his eyes. You've never really looked at them before, not right into them, as you find yourself doing now, and without thinking, you say, "Wow, you have pretty eyes."

This is how you start up with someone in an entirely wrong generation for you.

His eyes are green. He looks as though he could be Native American or Mexican; in fact, he is half Lebanese. He has long black hair and the cutest little mustache and Vandyke, both stubbly and barely there. He is big and handsome and young—how young? Shove that thought back under where it belongs—and by the end of the evening the two of you are making out on your couch. It's been a long time since you've made out with anyone. Go swoony with pleasure; feel as though your mouth has gone to the circus. Feel like an aerialist somersaulting above the crowd, a tiger leaping through a hoop of fire. Blue cotton candy and raspberry Sno-Kones and fresh apples dripping with soft caramel, colored lights whirling in your veins.

Somewhere between putting his tongue in your mouth and wrapping his big arms around you, he lets slip that he is twenty-eight.

You're fifty-four.

Fucking God.

Tell yourself you thought he was older. Mid-thirties, at least. You had hoped nearer to forty—there is something about him that feels world-weary—even though you knew this was pure self-delusion. But twenty-something, truthfully, had never entered your mind.

Say these words, firmly and loudly, as you pull away from him:

"You can't stay."

Get up and go to the bathroom to absorb the information that you have been lusting after someone about a minute older than your daughter. Think of the unfairness of it: why, of all the men out there, do you have to be attracted to this one? Remember the men you met online: the one who sniffed your armpit, the therapist whose diagnosis of sleep apnea for some reason precluded a second date, the lawyer who discussed the Ebola epidemic. Feel as though you have been given an adorable puppy and had it yanked away. Tell yourself you absolutely cannot sleep with him. Say to yourself, *Please please please please please.*

There is another factor to shore up your resolve: you have a vaginal infection. Last week you went to the gynecologist and mentioned that the one time you tried to have sex in the past three years, it hurt quite a bit. She wrote you a prescription for estrogen cream, explaining something horrific about thinning vaginal walls, loss of elasticity and moisture, and other things you did not want to know about the misogynist tricks that aging plays on the female body. You started using this cream, though you didn't think there was much likelihood you would actually need it. Maybe the cream caused the irritation. You also went out and got that one-shot medicine for yeast infections, just in case. Right now your vagina, along with being full of various medications, is itchy and sore.

Think about the word *vagina*, a word you hate. Why isn't there a good word for it, analogous to *cock* or *dick*? Good, strong, sexy words. *Cunt* doesn't do it for you. *Coochie, snatch, hoo-hah, twat, box, pussy, slit, gash, muff, beaver, Down There, fur burger, pink taco*—you want a new word. You want equality with men, who don't have to deal with mysterious pelvic dysfunction, who can just get it up (even if they need Viagra) and get off. Envy men their simple plumbing. Ready, aim, fire. If there is ever a cure for baldness, the disparity will be complete.

Pee and then wipe carefully, wincing. Imagine, but do not say, *You are so young that fucking you would practically be child abuse and I don't know if I can even have sex anymore and besides my pink taco is full of goo and I am as old as the hills, the ones that appeared three hundred million years ago.* Imagine wiping the happy expression in his eyes right out. Imagine him running off without his guitar. Instead, say this:

"I can't have sex with you. I'll drive you back to BART."

"Okay," he says. "But I'm staying over. You can't drive—you've been drinking."

"But all I had was a beer."

"You're small," he says. "It might be too much to drive on."

Wonder if you can muster the will to make him leave anyway. There is some strange force operating, rendering you incapable of saying the words, *Go home*. Think of asking him to sleep on your couch, or on the single daybed in your studio.

Let the strange force guide you to a compromise: he can sleep in your bed, but with all his clothes on.

Go into the bathroom and put on a tank top and sweat-pants. Insert a little more goo into your fur burger, both to soothe it and to stay strong. In bed, curl up away from him under the covers. Within minutes he moves over and wraps his arms around you, his twenty-eight-year-old hard-on nestled against your back. Lie awake most of the night, wondering what the hell you're doing.

In the morning, make espresso. Let slip these words: "God, you're cute." You've already spent the night with him; a little compliment, at this stage, couldn't make things any worse.

"You're beautiful," he says.

Drive him to BART before he tries to seduce you, before you mention your age and your hoo-hah. Make out with him some more at the BART station, kiss after kiss tumbling out like clowns from a tiny car. Greasepaint. Spangles and sequins. Watch him walk away, carrying his guitar, his long hair tied back.

THE FOLLOWING WEEK, he is at your door, a bottle of good pinot noir in hand. Someone has raised him properly, someone probably your age. Imagine you and his mother could be friends. You could hang out together, go shopping for cute clothes, and her cute son could take them off you.

Sit awkwardly side by side on the couch, like thirteen-year-olds. Soon his mom will drive you to the junior high dance, where you can tentatively hold each other as you slowly shift your weight from foot to foot while a band comprised of high school students blasts Led Zeppelin and Jimi Hendrix covers. Is he waiting for you to make a move? Remind yourself you are the experienced one. Two husbands and never mind how many lovers. Remind yourself that when you were standing in the Rockville, Maryland, courthouse reciting vows to your daughter's father, vows that would last about a year, this man was lolling in a playpen, clutching a tattered blanket, sucking on a pacifier.

Imagine sober, mature individuals urging you to come to your senses. They stand in your living room just beyond the coffee table, holding megaphones, saying, "MOVE AWAY FROM THE COUCH." Your daughter is among them. But it's too late. You are under some sort of spell cast by the Attraction Fairy. She has tossed her glittery handfuls of dust. It spirals down around you, clinging to your hair and clothes. You are trapped in a snow globe, two figures on a couch under heavy glass.

There is no escape. Not even Houdini could get out of this.

He has an old Acura his dad gave him. The paint is patchy, the front fender crumpled. Chili pepper lights and Mardi Gras beads hang from the rearview. The front bumper is held on with wire, the passenger side-view mirror with white strips of plastic. To operate the passenger window, he takes a straightened piece of wire hanger, sticks it into the mechanism on his door, and your window goes down. The seats look like an FBI

SWAT team stormed in there and cut them open looking for a drug lord's cocaine stash.

"Sorry about the seat covers," he says sheepishly.

Say: "I don't give a shit about your seat covers." At this point you are telling the truth.

When you finally tell him how old you are, say first, "I was born in a small town in Romania nine hundred years ago. I'm a vampire." See how good fifty-four sounds?

"I don't care how old you are," he says. At this point he, too, is telling the truth.

ACCEPT AN INVITATION to read at a literary festival in Ohio. The state, as far as you can tell, consists of two-lane highways, a lot of trees, and rain. Listen to the grad student driver chat with the writer in the front seat about Wittgenstein's propositions, Lacanian psychoanalysis, and the dominant aesthetic of the PhD program. Look out at the wet green trees and think about fucking your new young love.

Feel slightly separated, as though your molecules were scattering away from you in all directions, or maybe as though you were a sheet of Arctic ice breaking into floes. This is the Swoon: the early-stage chemical high that causes freak behaviors like staring into each other's eyes for minutes at a time and kissing for hours and, in some cases, disappearing together for days. Remember you have experienced the Swoon before. You know it is going to end one day, possibly badly. Think of the last time you saw an ex-boyfriend who was your community college student. You went to his apartment and, sobbing, gathered up a few things you'd left there, while he stared at the floor as though a small spaceship were going to land in that spot, hit him with a beam of light, and shrink him down so he could join the tiny aliens on their journey to a distant universe in which you did not exist.

You swooned for your daughter's father; you sat in his kitchen soon after you met, thinking *I want to have your child*, before you did just that. Remember sitting on a bench in front of a coffeehouse with him, feeling he was the best friend you'd ever had. When you got divorced, your best friend kept both the cars you owned rather than let the mother of his child drive one of them during the rainy season. Your second husband left you after nine months of marriage. He also left his eighty-gallon aquarium, which steadily leaked water onto the bedroom floor. One by one, the fish died. You took to driving over to his place and kneeling in front of his door, yelling curses through his mail slot. Later you got back together for a while, but then there was that little misunderstanding over your money and, once again, quite a bit of yelling on your part. Your new lover is probably too young to have a lot of memories of relationships that started in bliss and ended in the toilet. Possibly he is more optimistic about such things. Possibly he hasn't given any of this a thought.

As you cruise past more trees, past fake log cabin storage units and a billboard for relief from spinal compression, the conversation in front has moved on. Perloff, Sontag, Artaud, Homer. Feel like a blissful idiot, remembering your lover carrying you from room to room, your arms around his neck, your legs around his waist—an ape baby being carried by her ape daddy. Consider that if you had to, here in Ohio you could perform a few simple tasks, like signing the word for *food*. The parts of your brain dealing with higher cognition seem to have gone missing. In their place, little replicas of your boyfriend have taken up residence—one cooking you breakfast, another washing your dishes, a third playing an impassioned solo on "Pride and Joy." He's your little lover boy. He has unclogged your bathroom sink, enfolded your hands in his in a restaurant booth, given you a little inlaid box from Lebanon with prayer beads inside. You have history now.

The writer in the front seat is telling the driver how David Halberstam, the *New York Times* journalist, was killed. A grad student picked him up at the airport to drive him to a talk at UC Berkeley. They got in a car crash. Here in Ohio the rain is heavy; realize you may be killed any moment, in a similar fashion.

This is another thing happiness does: convinces you that your life is about to end. Feel glad you sent a friend the poem you wrote for your new love. At your funeral, she will hand it to him, crying. He will be devastated by your death, but he will know how much your brief time together meant. This grief and knowledge will fuel his art and make him a better man. He will love and remember you always and dedicate his first album to you. Though he will go on to love other women, none of them will stir his heart or move him as you have done. You will never have to pull out of the free fall, to take up the burden of a Mature Relationship. This you define as a relationship that has to be Worked On constantly, like a stretch of broken highway being repaired by a chain gang.

Think to yourself, *I don't want to work on the chain gang. I want to swoon forever. I want to keep flying.*

You are crying, sitting on his lap, your arms around him. Why does he feel like your father sometimes, when he is young enough to be your son? He might say you knew each other before, in a past life. He's a very spiritual person, in a non-projectile-vomiting kind of way. It's one of the things you love about him. You'd like to believe in past lives. Sometimes you feel that life is an amazing, perfectly tuned musical instrument, one that is also somehow alive, a beautiful, benevolent organism. Then again, you often feel it's all meaningless chaos and noise, everyone caught in a churning machine, ground under and recycled little plastic thingies that started out as humans and will soon become new trash bags or carpet fibers.

Wail softly. Say, "You're twenty-eight. Soon you'll move on. I'm just a part of your journey."

"Well, I'm a part of your journey, too," he says. "When I look at you, I see *you*. I don't see age."

Think, *Maybe he does see me.* Think of how you love everything about his body, even if it isn't perfect, because it's his. Love his scars and stretch marks, the shape of his hands, the way sweat streams off him when he's onstage playing guitar.

Be so in love you let him take you camping. Set up house, a tent by a river. Pee in the long grass among the cow pies. Lie on a blanket sharing wine and crackers, looking up at the stars. Take the mushrooms he's brought and float downriver on yellow inner tubes, coming on to the high, your body shivery and the grass and air liquid and the world a part of you, moving when you move. Be so in love you sleep on the floor on an air mattress in his sister's living room where he is staying now. Let him move in with you part of the week. Miss him on the days he goes back to his sister's. Travel with him to Seattle, where he plays guitar for your reading. Go to Lebanon, where you meet all his uncles and aunts and cousins, where you read in cafés in Beirut and see the cedars in a snowstorm during a harrowing ride up and down the mountain. Visit the village his father lived in as a child, and listen to the muezzin's voice floating the evening prayer on loudspeakers over the darkening valley. There used to be foxes; they are gone now. The house with the garden is a ruin. On Valentine's Day, go to the memorial commemorating the anniversary of Prime Minister Hariri's death from a car bomb in the middle of Beirut. A sign on a mosque bombed by the Israelis says, WE WILL REBUILD. Go south to see fallen Roman temples, to feed a small sick dog among the broken mosaics that resemble hearts, to try lamb's brains from a cart; drive north past the tin Palestinian shacks, then stop to eat fresh-caught fish from the Mediterranean and smoke apple tobacco from a hookah. Feel lucky to be there, to be able to be a tourist. Be completely in love.

In California, go to a barbecue and lie in a hammock together, looking up at the eucalyptus trees. The leaves are lit from beneath by the flames coming off the grill. Hot dogs, burgers, potato salad, pie. Kids and dogs roaming around, musicians setting up on a homemade stage near the house. Feedback. A twanging string. A field where horses move quietly through the dark. You're rolled up together, snug and safe.

Say, "Let's enjoy it now, before it all turns to shit."

Laugh.

FIGHT ALL THROUGH Thanksgiving as you cook a big meal together. Declare a cease-fire in time for him to put your dough initials on the crust of the pie he's baked. Not really your initials, but the initials of what you've come to call your alters, like the alternate identities in multiple personality disorder. His is a simple man named Pepe, easygoing and happy, a communer with nature; yours is Lola, a precocious sprite perennially turning five. Pepe and Lola never argue about money, or about whether one likes her wine a little too much or the other relies on his medicinal marijuana a bit too often. They cuddle and play card games and binge-watch TV series. Unlike Kim and her boyfriend, they are perfect for each other.

Remember a previous fight, the night of his birthday. He was turning thirty, and you were now fifty-six.

"Happy birthday, baby," you said, pouring yourself a third glass of wine—good wine you'd paid for. You often paid for groceries. You picked up some of the costs for his travel. Even a poet's earnings, compared to a blues musician's, are pretty substantial.

"I don't like it when you drink so much," he said, pouring himself a glass of wine, eating some of the chocolate cake you'd bought him.

"Don't tell me what to do," you snapped. You were often snappish when drinking. You criticized him, too. Truthfully, you were kind of a bitch after three glasses of wine.

On Thanksgiving, say, "Why do I always do this?"

"Do what?" he says warily, a forkful of apple pie halfway to his mouth.

"Fall for someone who can't give me what I need."

This is when he gets up and leaves.

After a few days, have a serious talk and decide to stay together. Feel hopeful all over again. Fuck the rules; you are an artist. You can transcend this age stuff and all the rest.

But really, you can't.

He leaves again during your final fight. He is a lot bigger than you, so it is impossible to stop him, despite raising yourself to your full five-foot-one height in front of the door and throwing out your arms. Phone him several times. Write him abject texts, begging him to answer his phone. Realize that your words are lost in cyberspace, never to be acknowledged or recovered. Realize you are alone in a vast, cold universe.

A YEAR LATER, attend a memorial for the blues musician who was your teacher in the band workshop. Your ex's band is performing. Go up to him and say everything you need to say: That you are sorry the two of you stopped bringing out the best in each other. That you wish him well. Hug him and walk away, hoping he is lusting for your ass in your tight jeans. Do not go home, drink some tequila and text him, asking him to come over.

He won't.

Wonder whether this affair was your swan song, whether you're doomed now to start piling *New Yorker*s and *Poetry* magazines on the furniture, to huddle listlessly in a moth-holed sweater in a dark apartment, waiting to die and be eaten by your cat. Your cat would likely not hesitate; she can hardly handle the hours between her late-night feeding and breakfast.

Quit drinking for a month. Make all your friends sick of you crying over your breakup, whining about feeling old and lonely. Write pages and pages of crap about him, crap you should be embarrassed to show anyone, and submit them to your agent as part of a memoir. Get rejected by every publisher in New York and a few scattered across the country. Keep writing. Wait, be patient; you will heal. One day you'll say his name and it will have only a little weight attached to it, instead of dragging you down into the pain and sorrow of love. One day, he will be your friend. It will be a tentative friendship on both sides, each of you aware of the harm you have done each other, each of you still caring, wanting to get it right between you, whatever it is. You'll go to hear him perform. Watching him onstage, seeing how connected he is to his music, how completely himself and alive, you'll fall for him all over again, swooning and starting to spiral. Later that night you'll walk with him in a park and stop by a fountain where you once held each other, and when he reaches for you, seeing the look in your eyes, you'll say *no*, and almost, almost mean it.

I ♥ New York

I was standing in the big renovated kitchen of my new Manhattan sublet one afternoon, making coffee, when I noticed a piece of cardboard sticking out from under the stove. Strange. I leaned down, pulled it out, and in an adrenaline rush leaped three and a half feet onto the counter and crouched there, looking down at what was on the cardboard.

Just a mouse.

I stayed where I was, trying to figure out if it was dead or alive. Then it moved, a little. It had a small spasm and then lay there, pulsing. It was stuck on a glue trap, firmly attached by its right shoulder and tail. The landlord must have put the trap there, not mentioning it to his new tenants.

Up until now, I'd been having a mad love affair with the city. It was summer, and I was living in a New Yorker's wet dream: two big bedrooms, hardwood floors, high ceilings, lots of light. I was hardly paying for any of it. My friend Elizabeth had a temporary job there and didn't want to live alone, so she was covering most of the rent. I was sort of a paid companion, a role I took to easily. I'd be very good at being rich, but no one has ever offered to test my talents in that department. I never made a dime from my divorces, not that either of my husbands had two nickels. New York was like a wealthy, handsome, intensely artistic, complex, slightly manic man who, for some inexplicable reason, was enthralled with me. Not that I'd ever met a man like that. Who needed men anyway? I'll take Manhattan.

It seemed you could get anything delivered here: pulled pork sandwiches, Thai or Indian food, beer at 4:00 a.m. when you were sitting around with your old friend coming down from the coke he'd brought over. I hadn't done coke since high school, and soon I remembered why: I hated the quick blastoff and the hairpin turn plunging you back down, a little lower than you were before. But being in New York made me want to be open to every adventure. *Just say yes* was my motto. I'd been living alone in Oakland with my cat and had concluded that I needed a change from my life in California.

Also, my daughter was in Brooklyn. I hadn't lived in the same city with Aya for ten years, since she went off to school in Minnesota and then moved to New York to be an actor. Now we went for coffee and walked around looking for vintage clothing stores. She stopped by between auditions. When she did a play in the West Village, I got to see it twice, in previews and again on opening night. This particular play involved her character being thrown around and nearly raped, so it wasn't the best one to revisit. She cowered against the wall a lot, looking terrified. She got slammed against it. The first time I saw the production, her bloody nose looked so real I wanted to jump out of my seat and save her. Elizabeth was completely traumatized. She didn't go out with us afterward, just headed off home, overcome and weeping. Such is the power of theater.

Washington Square Park, which I was always crossing on my way somewhere, was its own sort of theater: little kids and dogs sloshing through the fountain, a troupe of acrobats somersaulting over a row of tourists, a man playing "Moonlight Sonata" on a baby grand, about twenty-seven films being made by self-important-looking NYU students. When a man walked by meowing, I nearly fainted with happiness. New York was so interesting. When it got too interesting, I could hide out in the big lovely apartment while Elizabeth was away at her office all day.

Now there was a rodent. There might be more glue traps, more mice twitching on little squares of cardboard under the stove and refrigerator.

My coke-providing friend has agonized over killing fruit flies. He actually used to catch and release them, until they grew too numerous and he reluctantly bought a fly strip, after learning that even the Dalai Lama kills mosquitoes. I have no problem destroying flies, mosquitoes, ants, roaches, or other sentient beings smaller than my pinky. This mouse was considerably bigger.

It moved again and made a weak high-pitched sound. I got down from the counter and approached it cautiously. It looked truly stuck. My immediate impulse was to shove it back under the stove and pretend I'd never seen it. The mouse would die, and when the smell filled the apartment, I'd innocently find the corpse in Elizabeth's presence. She, being a former wildlife rescue volunteer, would insist on a proper funeral and burial. I'd light a candle, bless the unfortunate victim of urban progress, and recite a eulogy I'd written: "To a Mouse Caught in a Glue Trap." I could get a poem out of this. There's a solid tradition: birds trapped in airports or shopping malls or slamming into their reflections in windows. Animals getting shot or poisoned, flattened by cars, mangled by lawn mowers. I could use my mouse as a metaphor to explore humanity's relationship with animals. Or I could give my poem a political spin, and bring in class or race. I could make people really care about this mouse as an emblem for powerlessness.

I picked up the cardboard by the very edge and climbed with it out the window to the flat roof, where we weren't supposed to go. There was a glass door from the kitchen, but even though I'd spent an hour trying to pick the lock with a couple of paper clips, I couldn't get it open. I set the mouse down on the roof and tried, with another piece of cardboard, to free its tail.

This seemed to cause it pain, so I stopped. I climbed back

in the window, leaving the mouse out there, and watched it for a while. A smattering of light rain was falling. The mouse would expire in the open air instead of the dust and darkness beneath the stove. Or a predatory bird would swoop down on it. There were falcons in Washington Square Park. I hoped one would cruise by right now.

I went to my laptop and googled "free mouse from glue trap," though I wasn't sure I actually wanted to free it. If I let it go on the small, enclosed roof, it would have no place to go except back into the kitchen. It would get stuck on another trap, or else skitter around eating tamale and meatball crumbs. It would venture into the living room, then down the hall to my bedroom, make a nest in one of my shoes, and have tiny pink babies. Other mice would come over to see the new babies. Soon we would be overrun.

I landed on the PETA website and read, "*Glue traps cause slow, agonizing deaths.*"

By the time I was done reading the page, I was desperate to save my mouse. Cooking oil, apparently, was the way to go. I climbed back out the window and brought the mouse inside again. I found a long, shallow take-out container with a clear lid from an enchilada delivery the night before and cut the cardboard trap around the edges so it would fit inside. The mouse gave a little shudder. I spritzed it with organic olive oil spray, but the aerosol hiss terrified it into frantic squeaks and thrashing, so I switched to a bottle of Greek Extra Virgin, poured a little around the trembling body, and quick-closed the lid.

It surprised me that this technique actually worked. Within a few seconds, the mouse was free, sort of—anxiously moving around the small space, looking for a way out.

Now what? The roof? Not the roof. And I couldn't just let it out on the street.

Maybe it would peacefully suffocate now.

In the meantime, I really needed a shower. I'd been writing in my pajamas all day. I'd been in close proximity to a rodent. There were possible diseases. I looked at it frantically trying to find its way out of the container. What if it escaped to run loose in the apartment, spewing babies?

I climbed back out the window and set the container on the roof again, just in case the mouse muscled its way out. I texted a couple of friends asking them what to do. I called Elizabeth at work, but she was in a meeting. I wanted to leave her a message: "Call me back now or the mouse dies." Instead I texted her, *FUCK HELP MOUSE NOW.* "Fuck help" was our code for *"If you're ignoring me, don't—I really need you."*

According to the information I'd found, the mouse had about an hour's worth of air in there.

I went to take a shower and wash my hair.

In writing, getting away from the problem usually helps me find a solution, or at least a way to go back and tackle it again. In the shower, I decided on a plan: I'd take the mouse to Union Square, a couple of blocks over, and let it go in the park. I'd have to find a spot without people in it. I was not sure this spot existed anywhere in Manhattan. The people were as numerous as vermin. Union Square Park was full of them, pushing designer strollers, slumped on benches, playing chess, chanting Hare Krishna. Maybe I could let it go in front of the circle of those chanting, blissed-out, clearly insane devotees.

I went back out the window and stood looking down at the mouse. It looked up at me through the plastic lid. I could hear its thoughts clearly: *You are a flawed God, a cruel and unjust being who inflicts needless suffering on the undeserving. You are morally capricious. Narcissist that you are, you want everyone to worship you. The world would be better off without you. But right now you're all I've got. Please get me the fuck out of here.*

It was clear to me now that New York was going to test me, and not just this once. Outside it was summertime, and the living was privileged. Winter, though, would come soon enough, bringing record blizzards and dirty snow. The train would inexplicably quit running, and everyone would pile off the cars up to the streets, fighting for suddenly nonexistent taxis or setting off walking in snow boots and Eskimo coats. The homeless would sit on their corners, giant lumps of humanity buried under layers of clothing and dirt, somehow surviving. New York would come to seem like any other city, only with more of everything. Greater highs, grinding lows, more pedestrians restaurants nail salons students crazies pizza falafel musicals garbage trucks rainbow flags immigrant taxi drivers angry or jovial or indifferent; more town cars bicycle lanes No Parking trash bags small dogs in sweaters and impeccably dressed and made up old ladies. DON'T HONK. MAKE ART NOT WAR. PLUMBER LOST MY JOB

PLEASE HELP. CONSTRUCTION AREA. More TAVERN, BAR & GRILLE, WINE AND LIQUOR, HAPPY HOUR, COCA-COLA, HERSHEY'S, YAHOO!, WATCH THE GAP, YOU ARE HERE. More pigeons, roaches, rats, mice.

I put the mouse in its molded plastic prison into a Whole Foods bag and carried it into the park. I sat on a curb near some shrubs and flowers and waited. People kept walking by. They had no idea of the life-or-death drama that was unfolding, just as I had no idea about their lives, unless they were loudly broadcasting them in cell phone conversations. "Like at every like moment I was like, of *course* I'm not like taking a fucking like job as a barista," a twenty-something girl announced. Another girl with an earpiece said to the air, "At our age, dating is like going on safari." A man who was seeing a woman named Angel was confiding to the friend on the other end, and to me, that Angel needed to be beaten up when they made love or she couldn't come. As for the others, walking their dogs or children or hurrying toward some destination, they remained mysterious.

I pulled out the container, placed it on my lap, and waited some more. I felt too embarrassed to open it. My self-consciousness might have been the final nail in this poor creature's take-out coffin. It couldn't have much air left. I looked into the container. The mouse had given up looking at me with its bright, beseeching eyes or scrabbling around looking for an exit. It was lying down, still breathing. Probably not for long.

Finally I decided there was no way to set this mouse free

without at least a couple of people seeing me. *So what*, I thought. *This is New York*, a city teeming with weirdos, actors, artists, and every human desire and sorrow. No one would bat an eye at a woman hunched on a curb and opening her take-out container, a mouse appearing instead of a veggie wrap, seizing its chance, leaping fast as lightning into the flowers.

What Writers Do All Day

MOST WRITERS I know avoid writing. We bitch and moan about time to do this thing we've been called to do, and when we finally wrest that time from the maw of errands to be done and loved ones to be dealt with and actual paid work, like waiting tables or lawyering or reading other people's writing, we avoid it like mad.

I asked my four thousand Facebook friends—most of whom, of course, I don't know—whether they avoided writing, to see if what I've just said was true. A few of the responders said they didn't. If Joyce Carol Oates or Stephen King were my Facebook friends, I'm sure they'd be in that camp—though why would they be on Facebook, "liking" a photo of me gazing from behind a wineglass with a yellow smiley face taped to it, when they could be writing? One of my unknown friends opined with the force of holy writ, WRITERS WRITE.

NON-WRITERS TALK ABOUT WRITING. This sounds a lot to me like "Those who can, do. Those who can't, teach"—i.e., reductive bullshit. Good for him, I want to say, but for many of us, it's not so easy.

Besides, I like to think that avoidance is actually preparation—like a dog turning a few circles before it settles down in its favorite spot, or a tennis player warming up with some baseline rallying, followed by a few crosscourt forehands, down-the-line backhands, and overhead volleys. Preparation is definitely a better concept. So maybe listing what other writers do to avoid writing can not only demystify the creative process for the layperson, but serve as useful advice for someone out there aspiring to become a published author. In that spirit, I culled some surefire tips from my Facebook friends, which I list here:

> Try on your shoes.
> Hunt for obscure jazz CDs.
> Feel guilty and cry.
> Make lists of people who have died.
> Have sex, with or without company.
> Watch *Game of Thrones*.
> Load a bowl, pour an adult beverage, and then return to reflecting on the journey to the end of the night.
> Have a good poop.
> Work on your labyrinth.

Here is what I did for the last hour and a half of my scheduled writing time today: Wrote e-mails. Answered e-mails.

Texted my friend Donna telling her what I was making for dinner on Friday. Made toast. Wandered around my sublet in New York. Admired the colorful printed cloth I bought to cover a table in the sublet. Made a list of ingredients I needed for dinner on Friday. Checked my Facebook messages. Saw an ad for pillows on Overstock.com and took a look. Went to the Facebook News Feed and clicked on "25 Celebrities When They Were Young," from which I concluded three things:

1. Most people are ugly as teenagers.
2. No one is ugly in their mid-twenties, especially if they are destined to be famous.
3. I am old.

Wrote a lengthy e-mail, in my head, to the editor of my latest book. Did some yoga stretches. Wandered to the windows and stared out, thinking about how much garbage there is in New York. Wandered to the mirror and stared in. *Who are you?* I thought. *What are you doing in the middle of the morning when everyone else is out there selling sausages and gyros from carts, delivering FedEx packages, cleaning hotel rooms? Your roommate is a couple of blocks away, ending world hunger.* Elizabeth works for the Hunger Project. They go into poor villages in Africa and Bangladesh and India and empower people, especially women, to address their own needs and end their poverty and chronic hunger. It turns out chronic hunger kills a lot more people than those famines that get all the news coverage. My roommate was doing something about education and AIDS and potable water. I was still looking in the mirror, wondering what could cover those dark circles under my eyes. I was not a celebrity. I was a parasite.

Googled "useful parasites." Stared in horror at a giant close-up photograph of a flea.

After more googling, discovered there are worms that cause blindness or elephantiasis, that grow in your intestines, that can come out of not only the obvious exits, but also your nose and eyes. There are brain-eating amoebas and a blood-drinking catfish. Then again, parasites can help cure disease, be used to make dyes or ink, and help start a fire.

So, most days I spend a few hours trying to make something happen in language. I stretch out in bed, or on the couch, and tap away—dreams, rants, what happened yesterday, what's tugging shyly at me or having a tantrum trying to get my attention. I have organized my life around a belief in writing and a need to get it done, to spend long hours gazing up into the night sky of my brain, lit with memories and fugitive thoughts and propositions. Whatever the effects on the larger world, writing is a record of one consciousness trying to make sense of it all, or at least to transcribe some of the mysteries. It comes from showing up to the blank page, the empty file with its blinking cursor, and hoping the Muse will honor her end of the bargain and keep the appointment. What do writers do all day? Eventually, we get down to our true work, and keep at it.

Untrammeled

A NEW YORK photographer was doing a new book of portraits and asked to take my picture. His method was to give
his subjects black paint and pieces of butcher paper and
invite them to put down whatever phrases or images they felt
moved to create. The whole idea immediately made me sick
with anxiety. I can't draw, and improvisation is something I
try to avoid at all costs, even though I know that life requires
it on occasion. I did my best to plan, asking friends for ideas,
trying to think of clever things to do with paper and paint,
resonant lines I could memorize and then pretend to come
up with on the spot.

"Maybe I'll take off my clothes," I said to my friend Donna.

"Everyone does that," she said. "Do something original."

By the time the appointed day rolled around, I was

terrified. *I'm going to the shoot, I'm going to the shoot,* I told the part of myself that kept saying, *I'm not going. I don't want to be shot.*

I showed up at the photographer's studio, a space cluttered with tripods and lights and books and his photographs, and we sat down next to his computer to talk. Talking was part of the process. So far, so good; this was something I could do. We discussed books, the disempowerment of women, the juggernaut of technology, and the end of the world. We watched a few YouTube music videos. I even played a little harmonica along with one. I'd brought my harmonicas hoping I could have them in the photograph in some way, as protection.

"I thought I could spread them around me on the floor, or maybe hold one, or . . ."

"No props," he said.

Reluctantly I put them back in my bag. He led me to one side of the room where a white backdrop hung. The floor was covered with a sheet of white paper he invited me to sit down on. He handed me a small brush, a can of black paint, and several torn pieces of paper that had been crumpled up and smoothed out again.

"Take your time. Relax," he said.

I thought, *You are going to shoot me.*

Here's what I painted first, sitting cross-legged on the floor of his studio: a fat lady leaning out a window. I learned it in fourth grade, and it's the only image I know how to draw. It looks like this:

"This is all I can draw," I said.

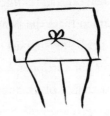

"That's a great start," he said, as though it were going to resemble a Caravaggio at any minute.

Now what? I was stuck. I was starting to sweat. Finally I painted I AM PARALYZED on another torn piece of paper.

"Creative process," the photographer said. "It's all about making yourself vulnerable."

Why would I want to be vulnerable with a complete stranger? I thought. *I have a hard enough time with people I actually know and care about.* The photographer gave me a gentle smile and went to fiddle with his camera. My brain turned over once, seized up, and went completely dead. So this was the goal of meditation: No Mind. My mind was as blank and rumpled as the paper. All that remained was a primitive, wordless desire to go home, where I could conduct my vulnerable creative process alone, the way I was used to.

The photographer wandered off to his computer to give me space for the next amazing thing I would produce. I sat there, occasionally painting a word or phrase. Periodically he came over to take a look, and then went away again.

Earlier he'd told me that some subjects had spent time crying on his couch before making their breakthrough. He had photographed a number of famous actors and artists.

Some of them had taken off their clothes. On his wall was an exquisite female specimen from the New York City Ballet, *en pointe* in nothing but her ballet slippers. That day, I was sure I would be neither a crier nor a stripper. Instead, I would impersonate an asylum inmate in a black-and-white movie, a catatonic in a padded room given simple art materials in the hope that she might reveal some clue for the doctor, some way to unlock a diagnosis. I realized that instead of my pretorn jeans and tank top and cowboy boots, I should have worn a hospital gown. Then I realized that what I was envisioning was a video, the one in the film where the little girl comes out of the screen and savagely murders people, who are found with their horrified faces twisted into sickening puttylike blobs. She's small and has a sort of black-scribbled hole for her own face, what you can see of it behind her hair that's fallen across it, and she's wearing a white smock of a nightgown. She is in deep psychic pain, and even though she is a child, you want to annihilate her.

The photographer came back and looked at what I'd done. "Good," he said encouragingly. "I like this one," he said. "Untrammeled."

I liked that one, too. I'd promised a friend I would try to use that word in a poem, and hadn't been able to. I'd thought it meant "untrodden," as in Wordsworth's "*She dwelt among the untrodden ways.*" I'd said it of my friend's forehead, because she thought she might be developing a line there, and I couldn't see a thing. Her forehead was perfect; she was thirty. "Look at that untrammeled brow," I'd said.

I told this to the photographer, who appeared fascinated

by the story of my friend's forehead. He gave me a pleased look and went away again. He'd looked just as pleased when I'd shown him my fat lady looking out a window, and I'd felt proud. This is how monstrous egos are created. Children who are applauded by their parents for every little thing—I worry about them. Those children are going to grow up believing they can follow their dreams, no matter how badly equipped they are to actually fulfill them. They will grow up thinking that working hard for something is what other people do. Most of them are going to fail and be totally unprepared for it.

I took another scrap of paper and wrote "Family Photograph" at the top. I wrote down my mother and father and the names of my four brothers, and then I drew lines through "*Mom*," "*Daddy*," and "*Jon*," who were all dead. I have an actual photograph somewhere, one of those black-and-white Christmas card shots with all of us sitting before the fireplace. My parents are dressed up, and my brothers and I are in our pajamas. I don't remember getting the photo taken; I was three. But I remember when my parents and brothers looked the way they do in the photo. Ever since my brother Jon had died the year before, I'd had that photo in my head. I imagined Death scratching out each face, maybe sitting cross-legged on the floor the way I was now, surrounded by wrinkled family photos, holding an X-ACTO knife.

I waited for the photographer to come back and tell me what a brilliant piece of art I'd created so I could get my picture taken and leave.

What I usually do when I get stuck in my writing, which is pretty much all the time, is to write "Nada, nada, nada" over and over. So I filled a piece of smoothed-out paper—it seemed more like a shard—with that word. The photographer came over.

"Hmm," he said.

"Can I paint on my arm?" I said.

"You can do whatever you want," he said encouragingly.

So I wrote NADA down my left arm in block letters.

Success at last. He came over, rubbed most of it off, and got behind his camera. He took several shots, and I loosened up a little. Maybe it helped that earlier I'd asked him if he had anything to drink, and he dredged up a shot's worth of vodka and one of rum.

"I like this idea of nada," I said, as if my opinion had anything to do with it. The alcohol made me expansive, as alcohol tends to do. If I drank enough, I might happily have taken my clothes off for nada, even though I would have regretted it in the morning.

"And what you did, rubbing most of it away?" I continued. "It's a double negative. It's ambiguous. It's like, nothing erased. You know, it could mean nothing is ever erased, like it all continues to exist somewhere in the world, or in another world. Nothing is ever lost . . . On the other hand, it could be the erasure of nothing—that is, something."

"Let's see what else you come up with," he said.

So maybe he took the photos only to fool me into thinking we were making progress. Now I was back to sitting on the floor, wondering if I could inveigle one more shot of rum.

I was painting five wobbly staff lines and a treble clef when he showed up again.

"Yes," he said. "This is interesting."

I added the notes of the repetitive riff from "Mannish Boy."

"Great, great!" he said.

So we were collaborating. Two artists in the midst of their creative process. "Mannish Boy" was written by Muddy Waters, record producer Mel London, and Bo Diddley. They worked together and created a blues classic. Look at all that was accomplished, throughout history, by collaboration: Lewis and Clark. Pierre and Marie Curie. Bob Hope and Bing Crosby. Masters and Johnson. Of course, there were also Hitler and Goering. And don't forget Leopold and Loeb, who got together and decided to randomly murder a little boy on their block, just to see if they could.

Please, I was thinking at my tormentor. *Please get behind your camera again.*

He took a bunch of photos of me holding up my crudely painted musical notes. Then he gathered up all the scattered words and images off the floor and handed them to me, and I clutched them in front of me while he snapped away, sometimes with a "*Yeah, baby,*" and at last it was over. I had not stripped and donned antlers as one poet had done. I had not drawn an enormous naked woman behind me and crouched down before her vagina like the famous actor, or fashioned a wedding dress out of paper like another poet. It was possible that whatever images the photographer had taken would never even see the light of a portfolio.

I thanked him, smiling my face off, and said good-bye. My left arm was a black smear. I took the piece of paper with *untrammeled* home with me. When I looked it up the next day, I discovered that it doesn't mean smooth or untrodden.

What it means is this: "*not deprived of freedom of action or expression; not restricted or hampered. A mind untrammeled by convention.*"

I taped it over my full-length mirror and took a photograph of myself.

The Process

I want to thank you for inviting me here to your low-residency MFA in Creative Writing Program and asking me to deliver the keynote speech. Shortly after receiving your invitation, I began thinking, with a mounting sense of anxiety, about drafting an essay for the keynote. I realized that I had nothing to say on the subject of developing as a writer, and that whatever I might have to impart had been imparted by others before me, more forcefully and gracefully than anything I was likely to muster. Quickly I arrived at a state of paralytic dread at the prospect of failure. I found it difficult to open the blank Word file on my desktop that I had optimistically titled "Keynote." Instead, I spent my time on YouTube, watching a clip titled "evil laughing baby," watching a kitty flush a toilet over and over, and teenagers high on Salvia hallucinate in a moment of brief bliss before a look of horror appeared on their features.

I knew that horror. How to face that empty file, that pristine field of electronic snow? It was so eerily silent there. It was a dead world, and I was its God. I might so easily fuck things up. But I had to begin, to find a first principle.

The first principle is simple: you just sit down to write. But this means finding time. And there is no time. There are the dirty clothes, the bills, the taxes (oh God, the taxes), that ominous rattling sound in the car; there is the dentist, the bank, the plane reservations, the Bundt pan—you need a Bundt pan! In an uncharacteristic fit of culinary zeal, you promised to make a chocolate applesauce Bundt cake for the potluck tonight! Well, fuck it, you will buy a cake, since the upscale grocery store is closer than the Bundt pan store; no one will ever know. You get gas for the car, drive to the grocery store, wait in line, have your debit card declined; you have no cash, your Visa was canceled last week and you didn't get it reinstated yet—fine, okay, whatever, store-bought cakes are a rip-off. You leave and go to the bank for money and drive across town for the Bundt pan and another day has run away like one of Bukowski's wild horses over the hills and you will pour yourself a drink before preheating the oven and getting on the phone with Visa to listen to that fucking bloodless automated voice. You have not gotten around to writing anything. You will begin tomorrow.

Tomorrow arrives, a wild horse approaching, its long mane rippling in a fresh breeze. You can do this! But you need space, quiet, and especially cleanliness, so before you begin, you must deal with the cat's dirty litter box. There is not only the clumped litter you have to remove, but also the mess of granules to be swept from the bathroom floor. Although you bought the covered box to avoid just this kind of mess, still the litter flies out of that little door. You really should dump all the litter out and scrub and wash the box—how long has it been since you did that? You keep meaning to clip the cat's claws, too—look at the state of the furniture. Also, the cat needs to go to the vet to get its teeth brushed, and the vet is open at odd hours. Better get to the computer and google to see when you can take her in. Then at least, you will be at the computer and can begin to write.

But while you are at your computer, 147 duplicate e-mail messages land in your in-box, and then your screen goes suddenly dark. You press all the keys, the On/Off, the Reset button: impossible, it was working a second ago, there are lines of a poem on there you didn't back up—you managed to write a little the other night when you were sleepless, worrying about your taxes at 4:00 a.m. You need the computer so you can write, and it is just sitting there stonewalling you, playing dead, or maybe it is actually dead, and what can you do? You stare at the blackness. You are helpless when it comes to computers. The Apple Store terrifies you. The cat goes into its box and pees and begins scattering the clean litter in all directions.

So already writing is not the easiest thing.

Then, assuming you are able to begin writing, there is the task of staying with it through false starts and wrong turns. The tone, for one thing: the tone is all wrong. You are supposed to say something encouraging, something useful, a cry to rally the troops. The tone is definitely wrong. And maybe the point of view. Is second person too affected? But you're so sick of the pronoun *I*. You are self-absorbed already, and using *I* makes it even worse. Maybe *we* would be better, more inclusive. Though don't you always just write about yourself anyway? No one wants to hear you whining about the litter box keeping you from writing. Everyone else has little kids, abusive spouses, demanding jobs, flooded houses in foreclosure. There are real obstacles in their lives.

And past those issues, you are going to have to say something wise, when in truth you are clueless. You are simply mucking around in the swamp of your overwhelmed life. Maybe you can mention Keats and negative capability, or drag in Yeats and the circus animals' desertion. No, scratch Yeats; the Yeats poem is about something other than being in uncertainties without the irritable reaching after facts or reason. It's more about writer's block—or maybe inspiration; you haven't read that poem in a while. Should you find it and read it now to make sure you know what you're talking about? Anyway, we're past that, we're on to the disaster of the next step.

Maybe your poem—this is you now, I'm trying out direct address—doesn't yet know what it wants to be about. Or the dialogue in your novel is stilted, the characters no more than caricatures drawn by some loser artist on the boardwalk. The memoir, fucking God, the memoir—this is me now, never mind you—there is so much, and how to organize it all? Where does my story start? Where does the part about my violent brother fit, and how to talk about my mother's depression, or that night in high school doing coke and wandering around the local golf course? Does that even belong in the story? Why can't there be a GPS for writers, a little electronic gizmo that says *"Your plot is going the wrong way! Turn here!"* Can't we all just go north toward bipolar disorder, make a U-turn at the Lodz Ghetto, pass our grandparents' feed and grain store, and end up with a lucrative publishing contract from a major house?

So, students, this is partly why you are here: to continue to find the courage to face down those days (sometimes weeks, months, whole years) when you can't get to the work. To sit down and write a draft, and then learn how to ruthlessly revise it. For the first draft is a wayward stepchild, and it is up to you to make it terrified of your footfall on the stairs, the rustle as you free your belt from its loops. You must beat it, sometimes within an inch of its life, no matter how it screams and begs for mercy.

But maybe beating the stepchild is the wrong metaphor. Maybe revision is more like math—because every piece has a particular set of problems, and you must discover the solutions. Einstein said that you can't solve a problem with the same mind-set that created it, which is why solutions sometimes hide from you for long stretches, or appear in dreams. Yet solutions are not integers; I don't know why I even suggested math as a metaphor. I despise math, despite having gone through trig in high school and even started calculus on my own with my teacher, but only because I suspect my teacher had a lesbian crush on me and was overly enthusiastic about my prospects as a mathematician. Why can't I tell you that revision is like an unfolding flower, each petal of possibility absorbing the sunlight of your skill and vision? Because sometimes it is exactly such a process, however scrawny the seedling. Yes, revision is a thing of beauty, a joy forever.

In order to nurture that seedling, you must learn the craft you need, so that as you keep at it, with occasional days off for weeping and despair, you can practice that craft. Mostly what you need to learn is to tolerate the mess you will make along the way, in the hope, not necessarily the certainty, that you will get to something better.

But maybe what you really need to learn is something else, like how to write a decent English sentence, and this may be the last thing you want to learn—you would rather learn the secret to ending a poem or story, the secret to structuring a memoir, and then go have a well-deserved beer and cheddar burger downtown in this godforsaken place. Of course there isn't any secret. Learn to write a good sentence. Even though you are in an MFA program and think that sentences are beyond you, or rather, that you are beyond them, odds are that some of you are not. If you are, congratulations. Skip on ahead and study structure on the larger level, which we'll get to in a minute. But be sure you understand concrete subjects, and active verbs that can carry a lot on their backs without being dragged down by hordes of hungry adverbs; choose one or two charming adverbs and give your gum to them, and them only. Know the difference between *its* and *it's*, between *lay* and *lie*: you *lay* the form rejection slip on the table; you *lie* on the bed filled with the anguish of self-doubt and feelings of utter worthlessness. Do not dangle your modifiers in front of any-one, especially potential publishers of your work. Learn paral-lel structure in sentences—read Whitman, and the Bible—and be able to write a single long, complex sentence that is graceful as well as specific, and be able then to vary the pacing of your sentences. Read Joan Didion and Denis Johnson and Lorrie Moore and anyone else whose syntax inspires you.

Still, you may lay down sentence after lovely sentence and follow them for months only to find yourself, in the middle of your journey, in a dark wood. Structure can still elude you. I don't necessarily mean the structure of a sonnet or Freytag's Pyramid of the story, though they are useful to know. I mean figuring out the structure to hold what you have to say, the best structure for the material at hand. The way in, through, and finally out the other end. You must, in other words, learn how to shit flowers. A poem or story or memoir, however gorgeously written, has to be able to stand up, and it will not stand up unless you structure it, unless you give it a skeleton. If there is no pattern, there is no art. Think hard about what holds your piece together, how the pieces connect, why and how each contributes. Remember that you are creating a world. Do not let it descend into anarchy. To hold anything together in life—especially oneself—is nearly impossible, but in art it is essential.

And remember this: if your heart is not a foul rag and bone shop, filled with lawn mower parts, a mummified opossum, and the dissected remains of your family and former lovers, you will seek a theme in vain. You may be able to buy one at the Theme Outlet Center, but it will not be yours; you will have nothing at stake. Have an uncomfortable mind; be strange. Be disturbed: by what is happening on the planet, and to it; by the cruelty and stupidity humanity is capable of; by the unbearable beauty of certain music, and the mysteries and failures of love, and the brief, confusing, exhilarating hour of your own life.

Probably you are doing all this already, or know that you need to, and that's why you're here, in this outpost of a state, far from the person or Barcalounger you love. You have a vision. The stink of the opossum, or possibly the Kodiak bear, is rising into the air around you, and there is something you absolutely need to say. No one is asking you to say it. You know that, and yet here you are, an army ready to do battle with the awful forces of silence. You have your weapons: pens and iPads and laptops. You are ready to hit the beachhead and march (or crawl, if you must) toward the hill to be taken. You are brave men and women. And there is no time. The hour is upon you; use it well. Carry into battle these words from Henry James:

> We work in the dark. We do what we can, we give what
> we have. Our doubt is our passion and our passion is our
> task. The rest is the madness of art.

Go forth, you mad and reckless soldiers, for the glory of it all!

How to Be a Dirty, Dirty Whore

STEAL A BOTTLE of Four Roses bourbon from your parents' liquor cabinet behind the bar in the rec room one night when they have forgotten to lock it. Your parents are upstairs in their bedroom, three split levels away, falling asleep in front of Johnny Carson. They have no idea what goes on in the bowels of the house. Call your friend Wendy and ask her to sneak out of her boarding school up the street and join you. Your parents almost named you Wendy, a terrible name, but Wendy is cool. She has been having sex for two years, and she is only fifteen. You, of course, are still a virgin.

Invite boys. The boys are friends of one of your brothers and friends of Wendy's, and you are nothing to them because you can neither supply them with pot, like your brother, nor give them blow jobs, like Wendy. At least, that's what you think is happening in the laundry room while you sit gagging down sips of bourbon on the built-in bench beneath shelves filled with your mother's tennis trophies: silver trays and mugs and loving cups, miniature gold statuettes serving tennis balls the size of frozen peas. You do not want to be like your mother, achieving early and astonishing athletic success, shaking hands with British monarchs and dating movie stars, and then getting married and having a bunch of useless, unruly children. You want to be Wendy: a hard-drinking, cock-sucking beauty with creamy skin and really good hair.

These are the first stirrings of ambition.

BRING FLOWERS TO your best friend, Marie, when you pick her up after her abortion. You are seventeen and still a virgin. You and Marie cut school frequently. You drive out River Road, past the mansions stranded on enormous green lawns, stoned and eating pastries stuffed with red jelly, laughing like battery-powered witch puppets. She has been sleeping with her boyfriend since she was twelve, but now they have broken up. She doesn't want to have a baby. No one you know wants to have a baby, not yet.

Go to a bar in Georgetown, carrying the fake ID that says you are twenty-two. There you will meet Chris, and Marie will meet Dave. Chris is the smart one. Notice that this is how you think: the smart one, the dumb one; whereas with girls, you think: the pretty one, the dog. Chris is a law student and has a southern drawl you adore. He is your first. It hurts and takes forever, and the whole time, neither of you can stop laughing. The two of you sound like a sitcom: short bursts of

guffaws and quiet chortles and occasional gut-busting hooting and howling. You will forget about Chris for many years,
until his friend from law school, who became your second,
gets in touch to let you know Chris has died. Notice how you
feel: like time has folded back on itself, a piece of paper on
which is written "My First Lover." Then the words are erased
with Wite-Out and a tiny brush.

YOUR FRIENDS GEORGE and Holly are older and more
sophisticated. They introduce you to Balzac, Nabokov, André
Gide, Anaïs Nin. You sit with Holly in the Café de Paris,
drinking Pernod, feeling that life is full of amazing possibilities. You read Nin's diaries and dream of becoming an artist, a woman who has affairs and writes erotica. George and
Holly have a friend in California who is a poet. There is a
world of artists out there and you want to be part of that, but
you don't know how. You begin keeping a journal.

FUCK DENNIS IN his dorm room at Georgetown University and have your first orgasm. Immediately jump up, run to
the pay phone down the hall, and call Marie to give her the
news, as you promised. Fuck Brian, and later Jack, in your
bedroom because there is a window they can climb in and
out of. Keep a list of the boys you sleep with and abandon it
after number ten. Fuck Andy when he comes back from
Vietnam, even though he wants anal sex and it hurts a lot.
Fuck some guy you didn't know was married; and Hank,

whose dog you like; and Fred, who once threw his TV out the window. Get caught fucking Conrad by a security guard in an empty room of the school where your mother uses the tennis courts to teach, the courts where you supervise the little campers in Group One during the summers. Sell tennis balls and string rackets in the shack by the courts and flirt with one of your mother's students. He is forty-something, and you are twenty. You fuck him on his couch while he fondles your breasts through your Café de Paris T-shirt, while his wife is who knows where. Fuck the guy building the toboggan run in the park, and a few more men you don't, can't, won't remember. Consider that the word *fucking* implies a fucker and a fuckee, while *having sex* is a more neutral and egalitarian term. Realize that in most of these cases, you were the fuckee.

ANNA SLEEPS WITH everyone, including you. You are both on acid. The walls keep moving closer, then farther away. Her breasts taste like soft-serve vanilla ice cream. She walks naked through the house during the party, like a deer stepping lightly through a group of hunters. When she goes out, men cross over three lanes of traffic to offer her a ride. She will be raped and beaten up repeatedly during the time you know her. Later you will hear that she has two sons, both in prison, and makes her living as a prostitute. You'll take out a black-and-white photo of her and study it. She reclines on a bed, her hair wet and combed back from her face, holding a tiny newborn white kitten in one hand and a cigarette in the other, harsh light on her face but her face itself luminous, ethereal, and calm.

AFTER YOUR FIRST abortion, write a poem from the perspective of the spirit of your never-to-be child.

FALL IN LOVE with someone who actually loves you back. Have a baby girl and try to find time to write while your new marriage falls apart. You are too young to be married, to be a mother, to know what the hell you are doing. You fall apart a lot. One day you pack the diaper bag to take the baby out, because she won't stop crying. Walking down the stairs, struggling with the baby, the diaper bag, the collapsible stroller, you drop the bag and everything spills out. You sit on the stairs and cry, along with the baby, for a long time. You have never heard of postpartum depression. That first year, you write a terrible novel, obsessively, pages and pages of unpublishable shit, while the baby naps, while she cries for you, while she smiles at you from her portable cradle, while another mother watches her. Then you leave your husband.

WHEN YOU MEET someone new, sleep with him right away. Wake at his place the next morning, hungover and disoriented. Do this only on the nights your ex-husband takes care of your daughter. The other nights, tell her stories about the little unicorn torn between her life as a wild animal roaming through the deep forest and her life as a princess in a castle when she is magically given human form. There is a prince, but no boy unicorn. Read poems to her: Keats, Whitman, Rossetti, Pound. She thinks the word *apparition* is hilarious; it sends her into laughing fits every time. Her favorite poem is Karl Shapiro's "The Fly," which begins, "*O hideous little bat, the size of snot.*" Her favorite picture book is Eugène Ionesco's *Story Number 2*, in which cheese is called music box and the music box is called a rug and the wall is a door and the ceiling is the floor and the mother's eyes are beautiful flowers.

Let her sleep in your bed. When you are sure she is truly asleep, cry.

A MAN CALLS saying he is doing a survey; do you have a minute? You sit down at the kitchen table while he asks questions that grow increasingly intimate. You should hang up. Don't. Put your hand down your pants and masturbate for a stranger, a pervert. Let him hear you come. Hang up and stop answering the phone for several weeks.

THE OLD ENGLISH *hore*, meaning prostitute or harlot, came from *khoron*, one who desires. But from the same stem came *carus*, dear. Cherished.

CRY AT OTHER people's weddings, drunk on champagne in the bathroom. Cry watching infomercials for Eagle Eyes sunglasses late at night, drinking gin, wearing a filmy white nightgown. Put scarves over the lampshades. Your second marriage has come and gone. It took nine months for him to walk out on you, as though his leaving were conceived the day you got married, the sperm of jealousy entering the egg of mistrust, spawning a furtive creature that entered the world and immediately scuttled away to the farthest, darkest corner. Your tears are flowers. Your sadness is a music box. Your second husband is snot.

STOP CRYING, FINALLY, and get over him. Write some books. Start learning the harmonica: Breathe. Suck. Blow. You can do this.

REMEMBER A NIGHT when your father, back from the bar at 2:00 a.m., opened your bedroom door and saw you sitting on the edge of your bed with a boy. The boy had taken off his shirt. Your father made him leave, then came back downstairs and called you a slut and a whore, advancing on you with raised fists. You scrambled back toward the wall. It was the only time he hit you.

When he was dying in the nursing home, you brought your husband-to-be to meet him. He couldn't speak, so you don't know how he felt, but his eyes seemed burning with some intent. You didn't tell him you were already pregnant with your daughter. You don't know, now, if the news would have made him happy or disappointed. Remember that when your daughter was two, you heard her talking to someone in the kitchen, even though you were alone with her. When you asked her who she was talking to, she said, "Grandpa."

REMEMBER THE PET names they gave you: Scrunch. Babycakes. Honey, Baby, Babe, Sexy. Love letters and long-distance phone calls. "I'll die if I don't see you today." One coming home from work and pouring rum and Coke and starting dinner. One composing on his baby grand piano. One photographing you tied up and naked. One teaching you about jazz. One lifting you up and setting you on your kitchen counter and raining a thousand kisses on your face. One and one and one, so many, but each man who mattered now with his own shrine, the images you keep close, the memories brightening, the lit candles of your words, your regrets, your gratitude for having known each of them. In a church in Italy you pay half a euro and light a candle for your father and watch it flicker in a row of other candles; no one here knows him, he's been dead for thirty years, but the flame is real, and present. The men you loved began with him. Most of them you have lost track of, but you can walk into your heart at any time and find them again.

FOR VALENTINE'S DAY, go out to an expensive restaurant with your friends Donna and Elizabeth. Wear your best black thigh-highs with the lacy tops and roses twining up the sides. Sit surrounded by couples, pairs of diners leaning toward each other, gesturing over bottles of wine. The wait-ress says, "What can I get you ladies?" Once you were girls. You ran around with your shirts off like happy savages until you got breasts. You spied on boys mowing the lawn, wrote them anonymous notes, called them and hung up on them. Boys sometimes asked for your number; other girls some-times asked to kiss you. Now you are Ladies. Now you are Women of a Certain Age, which no one wants to name. None of you has a lover. It has been a while.

Order the Amarone, the most expensive wine. Its name means the "Great Bitter," but what's in a name? Amarone is an elixir, cherries and plums and leather. Your conversation is filet mignon and baby carrots and amber light from the wall sconces. The restaurant is a chapel, an ancient stone farmhouse, a tent in the desert rich with rugs and incense and animal smells. Clink your glasses together: cathedral bells, telephones, a thousand wedding rings falling on marble terraces and rolling out to sea. Amarone grapes grow in poor soil, the roots digging deep for water. The three of you are drinking and laughing. You are unreasonably happy to be together. Happiness is always unrea-sonable, illogical, senseless, mad. You are the Charites, the Three Graces in Botticelli's *Primavera*, your garments diapha-nous under the orange trees. You're holding hands and dancing. It's spring. The walls are doors, the doors are flowers, and little blind Cupid has his eye on you.

Space

"Who is alive and who is dead?" my mother asked from her cranked-up hospital bed when I walked in. There was an IV in her arm and a box of Cheez-Its on the bedside table. The TV's volume was on, but so softly I had to look at it to be sure I wasn't hearing things.

She had a psychotic reaction to some drugs she managed to get hold of at her assisted living, Summerville. She wandered into the hall, pulled the fire alarm, and was carted off to Suburban Hospital.

"Well, Daddy's dead," I said. "And so is Gammy. And Izzy. That's it, I think."

"Izzy?" she said, startled. Izzy was the one man she had been with since my father's death twenty-five years ago. "Did I kill him?"

"No, he only died."

"Are you sure?"

"Positive."

"I'm going to be arrested tonight. You won't be able to reach me in the box. I can't make anybody believe me here, either. They really make themselves look human."

A nurse came into the room, picked up the chart at the end of the bed, and gave it a brief glance. "She's writing constantly," the nurse said. "She thinks she's been a very bad person and has hurt a lot of people, and she wants to confess. She seems very tormented. Maybe you should come back later."

"I'll stay," I said. I'd come again from California for a visit, expecting to see her at Summerville. I got back only two or three times a year.

My mother looked at the nurse. "You're one of them," she said.

"She's just a nurse, Mom," I said. "Mom, how are you feeling?" I wasn't sure I really wanted to hear. She looked terrible. Her left lower eyelid sagged. Her arms were blotched with bruises. Her short, gray-blonde hair was sticking up like a rooster's comb. I went over and hugged her carefully, avoiding the IV pole.

"Okay, not so good, how are you," she said flatly.

"Are they taking good care of you?"

"Oh, yes. How's your daughter, her dad—"

"Mom, how are you feeling?"

"Got any good—writing students?"

By now, well into her eighties and Parkinson's decline, my mother had her usual strategies of deflection narrowed down to a few repetitive questions.

"I'm here, Mom. You can talk to me. Do you want to talk to me?"

"Not really."

I stayed until she fell asleep. The next day, she was committed to the Geriatric Psych Ward at the University of Maryland Medical Center in Baltimore. The doctors had decided she was a suicide risk because of the drugs she'd taken at Summerville. It was true that my mother wanted to die, and I didn't blame her one bit. She was a mess. "Just pull the plug when I'm too far gone," she used to say, but there wasn't any plug to pull. She was stuck with living.

At the psych ward, the young psychiatrist who met with me and my brothers Gary and Rick suggested electroshock therapy. Our mother had been practically catatonic since arriving that morning. I thought that I, myself, would be catatonic if I found myself living on a gurney in the hallway of a psych ward, dressed in a peekaboo gown and slippers that looked like they'd come from a discount bin at the Dollar Store, with an orange band on my wrist that read HIGH FALL RISK and my name written on a piece of paper taped to my glasses. Also, it was a few days before Christmas. Locked into a ward with paper snowflakes and piped-in Christmas Muzak—who wouldn't curl up inside herself and wait for the nightmare to be over?

"Visitors may not be beneficial," the psychiatrist told us. She looked about twelve. What did she know about anything? We said no to the electroshock, and I got a room at the nearby Holiday Inn.

I sat at a table in the Holiday Inn lounge at 10:00 p.m.

with my notebook and a glass of wine. At the bar, two airline pilots were flirting with the bartender, telling her the Japanese phrases they knew. I wrote in my notebook,

Mom on psych ward notes.

I wrote down more crazy things she'd said, and phrases like *white matter damage* and *Lewy Body Dementia*. I noted that she was in Room 7, Bed 2, Ward 12A, as though fixing things in place—her words, her diagnosis, her exact location—could somehow change her circumstances.

In the morning I grabbed a bagel and coffee and went back to the ward. By the end of the day, she wasn't catatonic anymore. She sat in a chair in the room they'd finally given her, her gown pulled up, her feet propped on a chair, and I rubbed Curél on her legs. Her skin was practically transparent, like vellum. I could see the veins under the skin, like one of those anatomical drawings showing the circulatory system. When someone walked by in the hall I tugged her gown lower.

"For modesty's sake," I said.

She looked at me, and we both burst out laughing.

"I guess that boundary got crossed a while ago," I said.

We played gin, the rules for which neither of us could quite remember. How many cards were you supposed to have in your hand? How many could you just jettison? I read to her from a big, hardcover best-selling novel. Every sentence dragged along, saddled with an unhealthy load of clichés and adverbs. It was the writer's thirtieth book. It was likely she didn't even write them anymore, just farmed them out to other bad writers to keep the franchise going. This book was basically supersized fast-food crap. It was a McBook with no nutritional value.

"This is a good story," my mother said.

"Yes, it is," I said, though what I wanted to say was, *This is a terrible story. This story sucks. I hate this story.*

She thought the staff was poisoning her. "They look like they're human, but they come from space," she said. "I see them at night, coming down through the ceiling." When an orderly brought in dinner, she eyed the applesauce but wouldn't touch it. I picked up the plastic cup, peeled it open, and ate a spoonful, then feigned a sudden convulsion. This was probably not the best way to lighten the mood. For an instant she looked at me in complete panic.

"Just kidding," I said. "See? The package was sealed."

"I'm still suspicious," she said.

The next day, she said something uncharacteristic—that is, something truthful—about our family. "Daddy wanted kids, wanted a family," she said. "But then he couldn't handle it."

It was true that neither of our parents could really handle us. We were like those complicated gadgets you buy with high hopes, but soon grow frustrated trying to figure out. Then you stick them in the back of the closet. Also, the gadget that was their firstborn son was a little mentally ill, frequently malfunctioning, and attacking the other, weaker gadgets. Our father's strategy was to make himself scarce, traveling with ball teams or earning his plaque at the bar in the Touchdown Club in DC—Addie's End. Our mother's was to make sure she saw us mostly on the tennis court. Gary once dubbed her Wire

Monkey Mother, after the 1950s experiment: Scientists attached a bottle to a wire "monkey" with a plastic face. The baby monkeys got their milk from it, but they spent most of their time with Terry Cloth Mother, because cuddling was more important. This experiment made the monkeys crazy later in life, especially the females. They'd rock back and forth, holding themselves. They had terrible sex lives, and the ones that became mothers either ignored their babies or killed them.

But deep down, I understood by the time she was in the psych ward, my mother was all terry cloth.

"I've been a stinking mother," she said.

"No, you haven't," I said, and hugged her.

"I'm so afraid," she said.

"There's nothing to be afraid of," I lied, and hugged her again, holding her longer, feeling how thin and small she had become.

I went back to the Holiday Inn that night and typed up my notes, as usual, wondering what I was going to do with them. Who wanted to hear that my mother was really made of terry cloth? Who wanted to hear that a woman who had once been a champion athlete couldn't manage to button her blouse? This was life. It was hard to swallow. No wonder people reached for the salty, sugary crap that said everything was fine.

The next afternoon, we went into the room where the patients were being served lunch. Two conference tables had been pushed together. Everyone hunched over them, eating from trays of shitty psych ward food: Styrofoam cups of pea soup, mashed potatoes (probably the kind I grew up on, that came from a box—just add water), a damp roll with a butter pat, a chicken breast that tasted like an oven mitt, additive-filled vanilla ice cream in a cup. How was anyone supposed to get better on a diet like this? Next to me was a guy I'd heard earlier in the hall outside my mother's room.

"How about a song for you?" he'd said to the young psychiatrist, launching into a spirited rendition of "My Girl." After the chorus, he scatted a little, *oom-bah-oom-bah-dah-dee-dah*.

"That's very good," the doctor said. "And you're your own backup, too."

"I want to get out of here someday some shape some way. I need my dialysis tomorrow."

"You can get that while you're here. How are you feeling?"

"Except for a little headache, I'm feeling pretty good." He sounded cheerful.

"Let's wait and see how you do tomorrow," the doctor said.

That's it, I thought. *Today you're happy. Better wait a bit, though, since tomorrow you may be miserable.* What kind of philosophy was that? Why couldn't the doctor just say, "Merry Christmas"? It was Christmas now, Christmas on the psych ward, though there was no tree festooned with lights and ornaments, and no wrapped presents, no stockings hanging by the fireplace. There was no fireplace. There used to be one, in the house I grew up in. There used to be a family, dysfunctional though it was, our lives bound together under a single roof. Now the roof was gone. This, too, was life.

In the lunchroom, on a shelf, a radio was playing seventies music. The room was windowless. Clearly we were trapped in time and space. Neither Santa Claus nor Jesus was on his way anytime soon.

"God will put a star in your crown for taking care of your mother," the woman across the table said to me. She was wearing a fur coat on her head the first day I saw her. This morning she was spinning in the hall with her arms out, wrapped in a sheet and a pink boa. I had dubbed her Bling-bling because her top front teeth were all gold. For lunch she had changed into a green turban and flowing purple caftan. She looked regal.

I wanted to explain that I hadn't taken care of my mother all that much. I was just the daughter visiting from California. Gary was the caretaker. I was the writer. I would go back to California and try to put my notes into some kind of order, not sure what story I wanted to tell. I would think about reading a poem to my mother in the psych ward, a poem about my brother Jon's liver transplant ten years before, and how she cried, and how I felt I'd made a terrible mistake and caused her greater sadness. But then she wanted to hear it again. Jon was still alive then, and it was a hopeful poem, a poem of gratitude to the person who'd donated his liver so my brother could still have a life.

"Great," I said to Bling-bling. "The last star I stuck in there fell out."

"God doesn't test us," Bling-bling said, apropos of nothing, it seemed.

"What about Job?" I opened the mashed potatoes for my mother. They were encased in a black plastic container covered by a clear plastic bell. Without me there to open the thing, the potatoes might as well have been locked in a vault. My mother barely had the strength to lift her plastic spoon.

"Oh, Job was a good man," Bling-bling said. "They tried to get him to renounce God, but he wouldn't do it."

"But God killed all his cattle and destroyed his crops," I said. Actually, I couldn't remember whether God did these things or just let Satan do them, but what was the difference? If you tried the two in a court of law, God would be doing time, too.

A spoonful of potatoes fell on my mother's blouse. She didn't seem to notice.

"Also, God killed Job's children," I added, suddenly remembering.

"Well, he got those children back." Bling-bling was unshakable.

No, he didn't, I wanted to tell her. *He got other children, but that wasn't the same thing. What he lost, not even God could return to him.*

"God don't kill nobody," she said serenely.

Now the Spinners came on the radio. *Whenever you want me, I'll be there.* Bling-bling started singing along, so I did, too—though only on the chorus, because it was all I knew.

My mother dropped her spoon in her lap, mashed-potato-side down, and I picked it up and wiped it on a napkin and started to hand it back to her, but she had closed her eyes. She was shifting her shoulders a little, raising the right one and then the left, in barely perceptible movements. She lifted her hands just above the table, so they hovered over her meal like two little spaceships above a tiny city—maybe one they were planning to destroy, or maybe one they had come to in peace, to teach us how to cope with the pain and loss of life on earth.

Then I saw that my mother was trying to snap her fingers and couldn't, quite. But for the couple of minutes until the song ended, looking as though she were in a kind of beautiful trance, she danced.

Acknowledgments

THANKS FIRST TO my agent, Rob McQuilkin, for his savvy and his support, and to everyone at Penguin for true enthusiasm. To Elizabeth Sanderson for being an amazing and generous friend and roommate. To the also amazing and generous Marie-Elizabeth Mali. To my brother, Gary Addie, who understands the whole story of our family and has provided me with so many moments of grace. To the anthology editors who invited me to write essays that wouldn't otherwise exist. To Donna Masini for the photo shoot in her kitchen and for being beautiful in a million ways. To Susan Browne, for all the conversations before we die and are put into the Christmas tree forever. And thanks to my daughter, Aya Cash, whose love always, always sustains me.